THE BOOK OF CHAKRAS

THE BOOK OF CHAKRAS

Ambika Wauters

All inquiries should be addressed to:
Barron's Educational Series, Inc.
250 Wireless Boulevard
Hauppauge, New York 11788
http://www.barronseduc.com

Library of Congress Cataloging-in-Publication Data

Wauters, Ambika.
   The book of chakras / by Ambika Wauters.
      p.cm
   Includes bibliographical references.
   ISBN 0-7641-2107-3
   1. Chakras. 1. Title.

BF1999 .W38 2002
131--dc21   2001043182

QUAR.CHAK

Conceived, designed, and produced by
Quarto Publishing plc
The Old Brewery
6 Blundell Street
London N7 9BH

Project Editor: Tracie Lee Davis
Art Editor: Elizabeth Healey
Designer: James Lawrence
Editor: Andy Armitage
Photographer: Martin Norris
Illustrators: Mark Duffin, Coral Mula
Proofreader: Deirdre Clark
Indexer: Pamela Ellis

Art Director: Moira Clinch
Publisher: Piers Spence

Manufactured by:
Universal Graphics Pte, Singapore
Printed by:
Star Standard Industries (Pte) Ltd, Singapore

9 8 7 6 5 4

CONTENTS

INTRODUCTION SUBTLE ENERGY WITH THE CHAKRAS

This book offers the possibility of opening a new dimension of healing and growth for you. It delves into the nature of the human energy system and illustrates how our energy can be expanded and transformed through healing the seven major energy centers, also known as chakras.

The chakras are the key to physical health, emotional stability, and mental clarity. They act as conductors, filtering energy from the heavens and earth so that they can combine. The convergence of these energy fields forms a chakra. It is a vortex of moving energy, which then stimulates various endocrine organs in the body to secrete hormones into the blood system. (These are known as ductless glands, because their secretions go directly into the bloodstream.) The effects of hormones control our body. They also affect our state of mind.

Try to imagine the chakras as a "filtration system." It purifies our energy from the gross, physical plane associated with our primal instincts and basic animal nature, turning it into the highly refined, spiritual plane that connects us with the source of life itself. When we begin the journey through the chakras we open the way for healing, psychological development, and spiritual growth to happen.

As we progress upward through the energy centers, we learn more about who we are and the ideas and attitudes that form our lives. We are afforded the opportunity to enhance personal responsibility for our lives by transforming our energy levels. We become more intentional, more focused on the paths we choose in order to fulfill ourselves; we realize our talents and gifts and allow love and compassion to become the center of our lives.

Healing our mind is the same as healing our energy. We learn to love and accept what makes us unique, and to forgive ourselves for the times we diminished our sense of selfhood. We are able to transform our thinking about experiences and ideas by using our wisdom, and we affirm our worth and honor our choices for love.

This system of healing is ancient. It was mentioned in Vedic records and many original cultures embraced an understanding of energy. The Egyptians perfected it through the use of aromatherapy and color healing; they had an innate understanding of the soul of man and honored the earth plane as sacred. The early Jews codified their understanding of these principles in the mystical Kabbalah. In these early cultures energy was appreciated, understood and refined until a person obtained mastery on the physical plane and could ascend to higher planes of consciousness.

Today, in our highly charged world, rife with stress and glutted with chemicals—which we ingest as polluted air, poisoned water, and an endless assortment of allopathic drugs—we are in urgent need of understanding this ancient knowledge about energy and how it works. It strives to empower people to make optimal choices for health, connectedness, and love. It also teaches us that we are more than a physical body: we are a complete energy system that unites all levels of being into an energetic totality. What we think and feel influences every cell in our body. It contracts or expands our energy field and stimulates our vitality and the amount of resilience we have at our disposal.

Knowing how this system operates is vital if we wish to take charge of our lives. It puts us in command of our energy and helps us to experience our thoughts and emotions.

Right **Ganesha, the Hindu elephant god, is associated with wisdom. He is the protector and guardian of the Root Chakra.**

It helps us to change the way we do things. Being aware of the subtle and refined aspects of our nature takes us to another level of acceptance and healing.

As you read this book you will be invited to work with the affirmations, meditations, and exercises that have been created for all of the chakras. As you discover more about who you are, give yourself time to digest and assimilate your insights. They are your gifts of awareness and perception. As you acknowledge your desire to make your life more understandable and fulfilled, you may get a deep sense of your own purpose for being here on the planet at this time.

This book is designed to bring healing and joy into your life. It can help you expand your way of looking at your life and empower you to transform the negative and less wholesome aspects of yourself until your energy shines and you are the radiant light you are meant to be. Enjoy the process and be grateful for the abundant energy at your disposal for healing, consciousness, and light.

Right **Meditation is a valuable aid to looking within ourselves in order to reflect on a situation. It helps us to gain a broader perspective and more relaxed outlook on life.**

Opposite **There are seven chakras which are located up the body from the Root Chakra at the base of the spine to the Crown Chakra at the crown of the head.**

SUBTLE
energy

The world of subtle energy opens our minds to what we know at heart about ourselves and life. We live in the realm of energy, whether we acknowledge it or not. Becoming acquainted with it and accepting its effect on our body, mind, and spirit helps give us mastery over our actions, thoughts, and attitudes.

THE NATURE OF SUBTLE ENERGY

The phrase "subtle energy" refers to the force field surrounding all living things. In the human body it comprises the aura and seven layers of energy, which are referred to as the "subtle bodies." These control our physical well-being, emotional stability, and mental clarity. They are a direct reflection of our spiritual state and mirror how we feel about ourselves and life in general.

In this chapter, when we discuss subtle energy, we are speaking specifically about the human energy system and the way in which this energy animates the body and reflects our spirit.It is highly refined and easily differentiated. Subtle energy can be understood by the way it affects our emotions, our thinking, and our physical health.

A person trained in subtle-energy work can distinguish its various components through extrasensory perception, dowsing, or touch. Diagnosis of disease or negative mental attitudes can be done by looking at the chakra system and the aura to bring clarity and focus to the various life challenges and emotional issues related to that person.

It is important to understand that even though this energy is not visible it can be experienced. It is apparent in people and can be felt by the light, open quality they have or by their negative demeanor. Even though we cannot see their energy, we perceive the quality of their energy field through their body language, the brightness or dullness in their eyes, the clarity or confusion of their minds, and, by the things they say and do. Subtle energy pervades every interaction we have with people, plants, and animals. It is the life force exchanged between us.

EXPERIENCING SUBTLE ENERGY

This is one way in which you can experience subtle energy. Begin by rubbing your hands briskly together and holding them a few inches from one another. Feel the heat that emanates from them. That heat is "subtle" energy. It can be used for healing pain, emotional dysfunction, and mental imbalance. It is imprinted with your spirit and the thoughts and feelings you have. The more positive your thoughts, the stronger your energy field.

The Aura

The aura is the energetic envelope that sheathes the body of any living thing. It acts as a bubble to enclose the energy field and protect the life force. It is the encasement that enables energy to circulate through living systems.

The layers of atmosphere form an aura of energy that keeps oxygen in circulation. Its purpose is to ensure life, so that we can breathe, and it keeps out harmful rays from the sun.

When the aura is weakened by disease or distress, it is unable to hold its full capacity of energy. An example is the hole in the ozone layer, which allows harmful ultraviolet radiation into the atmosphere. A compromised aura in the human energy system does something similar when it is distressed.

Having a strong and viable energy field insures against external invasion, which can take the form of psychic attack and even physical disease. If our aura is weak, we can strengthen it with positive thinking, meditation, and prayer. Energy follows thought and responds immediately to our intentions. Living a healthy lifestyle also builds a strong auric field.

In humans the aura is made up of several layers of subtle energy. There are seven energy bodies in total that affect every state of our being. Each layer acts as a filter for life energy. They exist at a gross, physical level and proceed to more differentiated and refined layers of energy.

Energy moves up from the earth into our lower chakras and affects our physical bodies. It anchors our spirit in the material reality. It also moves down from the cosmos through our upper chakras and affects our thinking, feelings, and spiritual perception.

Our energy fields are transformed as our consciousness develops. The more we connect with the absolute oneness of life, the stronger our subtle energy becomes. We can transform our energy through awareness and by understanding how the life force responds to positive intention.

Opposite **Subtle energy is all around us. It pervades all nature, and infuses the etheric realms of life with vitality and life force.**

Below **The colors of the rainbow are the same as the sequence of colors in the chakras of the Human Energy System. Red has the densest energy and corresponds to the magnetic earth energies, while violet, which is the least dense, relates to the electric, cosmic end of the spectrum.**

THE SEVEN LAYERS OF THE AURA

The layers of the aura correspond to the seven planes through which we have our being. From the top down they are the Divine, the Monadic, the Spiritual, the Mental, the Emotional, the Etheric and, finally, the Physical. All these bodies are enveloped within the auric sheath. This sheath is called the condula.

Each plane is divided into seven sub-planes, giving us 49 planes of energetic activity in all. The highest plane is the Divine plane, where the Godhead is experienced. Below it is the Monadic plane, which is the vehicle the soul uses to express itself. It is said that the soul uses the lower planes to develop experience and maturity for its growth and healing.

The Spiritual body functions as a conduit to our higher aspects through meditation, prayer, and inner reflection. The Mental body is made up of our attitudes about life.

The Emotional body opens up as we become more sensitive and trust our feelings to act as inner guidance. It corresponds to our awareness of Self as valuable and good, worthy of love, kindness, and respect. It is made up of our desires and, as a result of our incessant longings, is very volatile. It is in this plane that disease originates that can deeply affect our physical health. It is through the Emotional body that we experience the range of opposites such as pleasure and pain, fear and courage, attachment and disengagement. This is where energy gets blocked and imploded when our all-consuming desires run our lives.

The Etheric body is the thickest and densest of the subtle bodies. It vitalizes and energizes the Physical body and connects us with the cycles and rhythms of earth energy. The chakras exist in this layer of energy, next to the Physical body. The chakras stimulate the ductless glands (endocrine organs that are known as ductless glands because they secrete directly into the bloodstream) of the Physical body, which produce different states of health, depending on our feelings and attitudes. The Physical body contains all our organic systems and is composed of gases, liquids, and dense matter. It is on this plane that the spirit can express itself, learn the lessons of life, and cultivate wisdom.

All the bodies interact within themselves. They are highly differentiated fields of energy where our spirit, our feelings, and our body act as one. Body/mind/spirit is one continuum without separation.

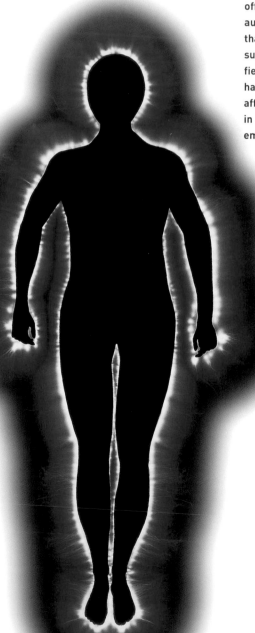

Opposite **The atmosphere surrounding Earth holds in vital gases that sustain life on our planet. The aura acts in a similar way by enveloping our vital life energy so that we can grow, thrive, and develop to our fullest potential.**

Below **Kirlian photography was developed in the 1930s. While it does not offer an image of our auras, it demonstrates that every living thing is surrounded by an energy field. This energy field has been shown to be affected by changes in physical and emotional states.**

VISUALIZING THE AURA

Imagine a photo of the planet Earth with layers of atmosphere surrounding the globe. These layers hold the vital levels of essential gases needed for life. Without an energetic envelope surrounding the planet there would be no atmosphere. Our planet would be bare and without life.

Visualize the same sort of envelope around your body. It extends about eight inches (20 cm) from the surface of your body. It contains all the vital energy you need to live. You can expand this field by thinking very positive and loving thoughts, such as "I am love" and "I love myself," repeatedly. You can also shrink this field by thinking negative thoughts about yourself. Each time you affirm your being, you contribute to your overall health and well-being.

You can attempt to visualize the entire planet embraced within your auric field. This way you are one with all life. Doing this visualization daily will expand your aura. If you practice in front of a mirror, you may be able to see your energy field form around your head and chest. This atmospheric layer expands and contracts as a response to your thought forms.

THE HUMAN ENERGY SYSTEM

The human energy system comprises seven layers of energy bodies within the aura. The chakras exist in the first layer of subtle energy and influence our physical, emotional, and mental states. They act as conductors for energy to move through all layers of the aura. Their health and integrity are maintained through a grounded lifestyle and positive and loving thoughts toward the self and the surrounding world.

The word chakra comes from the ancient Sanskrit and means "wheel of light." It refers to the energy around and within all life forms. Chakras are a model that describes the subtle levels of energy.

It is said that minerals and crystals contain one chakra that conducts energy in and out of their living substance; animals have up to three chakras; and human beings presently have seven major chakras and twenty-one minor chakras, and all the acupuncture points also act as chakras. As we continue to evolve and become more sensitive to energy, we will cultivate new chakras to process refined energy layers.

This manner of comprehending energy is based on the ancient knowledge that all life is energetic and spiritual in origin. The ancients modeled the chakra system on a complete acceptance that man and Earth were one and inseparable. Each chakra, or energy center, is linked to an element. The earth element, for instance, is associated with the Root Chakra. This chakra sits at the base of the spine and conducts energy into the hips, legs, and feet. It connects us to Earth and its field. Through the Root Chakra we are anchored physically in our bodies and supplied with the life force we need to maintain and support our lives.

Each chakra corresponds with many different qualities and substances. For instance, each chakra resonates with a color and a musical note. We find affinities to specific crystals, gemstones, and even plants. The ancients made up myths to

connect the chakras with archetypal characteristics so that people could understand the life issues and qualities that were associated with each vital life center.

The chakras comprise various levels of awareness, activity, and energetic charge. For instance, the Root Chakra is red and has a very dense vibration. It affects our ability to be present in our body and produces the vitality that we need to stay alive. Toward the other end of the energy spectrum, the Brow Chakra vibrates to affect our mental and spiritual processes. It resonates with a different musical note and has an affinity to the color blue.

The lower chakras fall into the category of magnetic energy, whereas the upper chakras are electrical in nature. The lower three chakras, which sit below the diaphragm, are known as the feminine chakras in that their function is specifically receptive. They take in energy from the earth and the immediate environment.

Opposite **The chakras are an ancient model that describe the human energy system in its various components. This model originated in India perhaps as long as 25,000 years ago.**

Below **Chakra means "wheel of light" and refers to the spinning vortex of energy created when magnetic energy from the molten core of the earth rises up and meets electric energy descending from the cosmos. This wheel, made up of both these forces, propels our life force.**

They link us with Mother Earth and the events and qualities that tie us to family, clan, tribe, and community. They concern themselves with how we master life through our instincts, using inherited ancestral energy to maintain our life force. These chakras also carry the patterns for disease and health, as well as the courage, cunning, and stealth required to stay alive.

The upper four chakras are known as the masculine chakras. They are primarily concerned with giving energy out in the form of love, communication, healthy attitudes, and inner reflection. They link us with the source and become active as we become spiritual and capable of love. These chakras are all interdependent. When one energy center is shut down, others will compensate in maintaining the life force. They have defined boundaries that distinguish one from another. The various parts of the energy system are interlinked to maintain the continuum of life.

CHAKRA
functions

The chakra system is a model
for the flow of energy that runs
through all life and through the
human energy system. It is like
a ladder that takes us from the
physical realm of substance up
through the workings of the
higher mind and spirit, and into
the realm of Divine
Consciousness.

THE CHAKRAS

Chakras are nonanatomical in nature. They exist in the energy body known as the Etheric body, which, as we have seen on page 12, is the layer of energy closest to the Physical body.

The chakras penetrate all seven layers of the aura. They act as conductors, drawing vital energy up from the earth, circulating it through the Physical body, and releasing it as higher awareness. In other words, vitality is transmuted into awareness, spirituality, and a deeper conception of the universe. Likewise, cosmic energy moves down through the Crown Chakra and manifests as right action, creativity, and health.

As we develop our consciousness and refine our sensitivities, we release old, stagnant emotional energy in the form of dreams, memories, and feelings that weigh down our spirit. The more freedom, love, and beauty the spirit experiences, the wider the energy fields become. As we evolve, we actually become healthier, with more energy available to us for healing, creativity, and joy.

The process of opening up to greater energy fields occurs as we live fully in the present. The state of our chakras is very important. They are the vital key to what we think and feel, as well as the accumulated dross of our past. They are the ladder of love that takes us from the lowest and most base aspect of life, which is concerned with survival, to the highest realm of consciousness, healing, and bliss.

Our chakras are the repositories of our thought, feelings, and attitudes about life. If we have narrow ideas about life and limit our existence, then our energy field will be small and narrow. Without the adequate amounts of vital energy, we fall into physical and psychological imbalance. Chronic shortages of energy lead to illness and death.

Above **All energy moves in spirals. This wheel describes the dynamic action of energy in the chakras. Water is the element that governs the function of the Sacral Chakra, and has a strong affinity with our emotions.**

HOW THE CHAKRAS FUNCTION

The chakras form a well-organized system that keeps the life force directed, economical, and fluid. When something happens to impede the flow of life energy, the chakras slow down activity, and energy becomes sluggish and even stagnant. If this situation is temporary, the energy resumes its natural flow. If the situation continues for some time, the chakras need stimulation to become active again. Our health and well-being depend on active chakras.

ROOT CHAKRA

The first of these energy centers is called the Root Chakra. It rests in the perineum at the base of the spine, and draws energy from the magnetic field at the earth's core. This energy moves up through the feet and legs, energizing blood and tissues in the body. It stimulates aggressive drives linked to survival, and anchors our spirit on the material plane, establishing our worldly existence.

On a physical level, this chakra controls the adrenal cortex (on the upper end of each kidney), which is the storehouse for inherited ancestral energy. The Root Chakra holds both our genetic inheritance for vitality as well as our innate predispositions to disease. Within this domain are stored the qualities that helped our ancestors survive, such as courage, stamina, and resilience.

The Root Chakra also governs the birthing process. The ability to nurture life depends partly upon a woman's acceptance of her physical nature and her instincts for survival. If there are emotional issues about control or fear, the birthing process may be an ordeal. A good connection with the Root Chakra helps a woman to have a normal birth.

In its unconscious state, the Root Chakra carries the attitudes and prejudices formed by family, church, and culture. As these barriers are erased through developed awareness, more energy is available to live the life you choose.

SACRAL CHAKRA

The next chakra is the Sacral Chakra, located in the pelvis, near the sacrum. This energy center promotes our ability to enjoy life in physical ways. It governs our vital well-being, our sense of deserving of a good life, and our capacity to develop a sense of abundance.

The Sacral Chakra controls our physical ability to move forward in life. It is governed by the water element, and affects emotions, which, if unexpressed, can cause fluid retention in the body.

This chakra is deeply influenced by our ideas about pleasure and our sense of our own sexuality. Being in touch with our sexual drives and discerning in our sexual behavior allows us to grow emotionally. Wholesome attitudes about sexuality offer us the promise of fulfillment, joy, and a deep and abiding connection with another.

The Sacral Chakra's function is contingent upon the degree we care for and value our own being. If we feel we are deserving of the good things around us, this chakra opens to receive pleasure and abundance. If we doubt our right to pleasure, this chakra becomes depleted. It also controls the appetite, and its lesson revolves around knowing what is enough.

The Sanskrit word for this chakra is *Swvatistana*, which translates as "my own sweet abode." It refers to our ability to cherish our physical presence and to find pleasure, health, and joy.

SOLAR PLEXUS CHAKRA

The third energy center is the Solar Plexus Chakra. It sits over the stomach and the nerve ganglia under the diaphragm. It filters energy into our vital organs so that they can break down nutrients for digestion. This happens on the physical level with food and on the mental level with ideas.

Above **Swvatistana means "my own sweet abode" in Sanskrit and refers to the Sacral Chakra, located in the center of the pelvis. This is where pleasure, deservability, well-being, and abundance are anchored in the body.**

This center is directly related to self-value, a primary quality in our relationships with others and the world around us. If we fail to honor ourselves and know that we are worthy simply because we exist, our sense of personal identity is weak. Consequently this chakra deals with self-esteem, confidence, and freedom of choice. It reflects how we see ourselves and exercise our innate power.

The Solar Plexus Chakra is ruled by the element of fire. This is the energy of passion, which affects how we approach the world. It controls our basic instincts in our relationship to events and people.

Living within the trap of self-limitation, this chakra reduces its energy for expressing power. Demeaning ideas prevent us from gaining an education, establishing financial stability, and achieving independence. We all have a right to a strong and healthy sense of ourselves and to live our own lives.

Above **Fire is the element that rules the Solar Plexus Chakra. This is named for the Sun and is the center of our sense of personal identity. As the physical body uses this chakra to break down food into usable nutrients using heat, so the lower mental body found in the Solar Plexus breaks down ideas for us to assimilate mentally for our growth and development.**

HEART CHAKRA

The Heart Chakra is the center of the human energy system. It functions both physically and emotionally to keep the life force alive. Just as the heart organ carries the life blood through the body, so the Heart Chakra moves love through our lives.

The Heart Chakra operates on the physical as well as the emotional and energetic planes. Physically the heart comprises the myocardium, the aorta, the pulmonary artery, and the four chambers. Energetically, it comprises the heart protector, which shields it from emotional pain, and the spiritual heart, which is pure and thought to be the seat of divinity within us.

The heart thrives on brotherhood, joy, peace, and understanding. A happy heart is the tonic of life. Gradually we mature and need to take less. Instead we give love unconditionally. This new form of love is inclusive and universal. It rests on our ability to avoid hurting others, and our compassion for those who suffer.

THROAT CHAKRA

The Throat Chakra covers the area of the external and internal throat and neck as well as the mouth, teeth, and jaw. It is often blocked with suppressed feelings, revealing unspoken emotions and unexpressed ideas. When the Throat Chakra is blocked, it prevents energy from rising to the upper centers. Clearing this center requires a deep commitment to the truth, as well as living from integrity. When it is healed, strength flourishes and directs the life force toward creativity and self-expression.

The qualities expressed by the Throat Chakra are creativity, willpower, the truth, communication, and personal integrity. This center governs the thyroid and controls our ability to communicate our thoughts, feelings, and ideas clearly. When the Throat Chakra is functioning optimally, people will take stands for what they believe in. They are seldom dependent on others to give them permission to express their feelings.

This chakra develops later in life when a person has maturity to know what really matters. Clearing out family suppression and unexpressed emotions takes many years of inner work. This chakra holds memory and energy of all that went unexpressed. It is deeply affected by substance abuse, gossip, lying, and lack of personal integrity.

BROW CHAKRA

The Brow Chakra sits between the eyebrows and is known as the Third Eye. This center is our innate intelligence and thrives on the distilled wisdom of our losses, pain, and separations. When it is open and functioning well, we can discern our highest good as well as profound awareness and intuition. The center seeks meaning, truth, and freedom.

The Brow Chakra controls the flow of hormones from the pituitary gland and responds to wholesome attitudes about self and others. As we mature we cultivate knowing and intuition and use these to understand situations we might not have been able to cope with when we were younger. Wisdom, discernment, knowledge, and intuition are all qualities of this chakra. It is closely linked with the higher mind and enlightenment.

CROWN CHAKRA

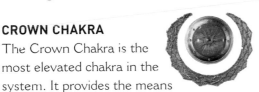

The Crown Chakra is the most elevated chakra in the system. It provides the means to deepen our indelible connection with the source of our being. Whether we wish to make this connection conscious is up to us.

The link is there; we must only acknowledge it to experience it. There is nothing to be done to make this connection other than recognize it.

The Crown Chakra controls the pineal gland, which sits at the top of the midbrain below the cerebral hemisphere. It influences our deep inner cycles, such as sleep, happiness, and tranquility. Its qualities are bliss, beauty, and spirituality. The Crown Chakra offers each person the energy of cosmic consciousness and helps us feel that we are one with all life. It controls our sense of happiness and joy and allows us to feel that we are loved, guided, and protected at all times by the love of God.

ARCHETYPES AND CHAKRAS

Archetypes have emerged out of the core of human experience to represent the good and bad qualities in us all. Each archetype symbolizes a quintessential pattern of energy that describes a set of fixed patterns of behavior. In the case of the chakras, each archetype refers to a level of personal responsibility, a degree of empowerment, and a quantity of energy and vitality. Each chakra has a positive archetype and a negative one, corresponding to the qualities and challenges associated with that chakra.

These archetypes are transformed by conscious awareness. The more responsibility we take for our personal archetypes, the more empowered we are and the more energy we have available for our health, creativity, and joy. Recognizing our negativity opens the chakra and psychologically empowers us and revitalizes our health. When we begin to take responsibility for the negative attitudes that block our aliveness and happiness, we heal an aspect of ourselves and move onto higher ground.

CHAKRA	NEGATIVE	POSITIVE
ROOT	The Victim: Lacking energy, empowerment and life force	The Mother: Nurturing, self-sufficient, responsible
SACRAL	The Martyr: Critical, sour, condemning	The Emperor/Empress: Pleasure, abundance, enjoyment
SOLAR PLEXUS	The Servant: Needy, seeking approval, unempowered	The Warrior: Confident, creative, courageous
HEART	The Actor: Conditional love, bound by convention	The Lover: Generosity, openness , loving, good will
THROAT	The Silent Child: Suppressed communication, unexpressed emotions	The Communicator: Outspoken, truthful, open
BROW	The Intellectual: Rational, factual, rigid, dry	The Wise Person; Flexibility, humor, cultivation of wisdom
CROWN	The Egoist: Arrogance, self-absorption, inflexibility	The Guru: Cultivation of grace, bliss, gratitude. Acknowledging divine intervention

THE CHAKRAS AND THE PHYSICAL BODY

The vital force of the human energy system directs energy through the layers of subtle energy bodies. It is the living part of us that moves our limbs, and lets us feel emotions and make free choices. It animates our minds and preserves us under stress. The vital force exists in all life forms and is the same whether found in a human being, an animal, or a plant. It is differentiated by form but is the same force in all living things. It distinguishes life from nonlife.

This force directs our physical energies, using the chakras as conductors to filter energy through the physical body. Energy moves through the chakras, stimulating hormone flow in the ductless glands. These, in turn, affect the biochemistry of the body and the rate at which the body uses energy. At a physical level this is called metabolism.

When our body stores excess heat or fluid, it affects the way the body processes energy. Too much heat, which may be

THE CHAKRAS:

ROOT CHAKRA
Ductless gland: **adrenal cortex**
Associated body parts: **kidneys, blood, the skeletal system**
The physical problems of the Root Chakra are conditions that affect the feet, knees, and hips, including arthritis, kidney stones, osteoporosis, bone problems, and autoimmune deficiency conditions.

SACRAL CHAKRA
Ductless gland: **ovaries in women/testes in men**
Associated body parts: **sex organs, bladder, uterus in women, prostate in men**
Dysfunction of the Sacral Chakra in women can create endometriosis, as well as sterility, chronic menstrual cramping, fibroids, and problems with ovaries and cervix. In men it can create prostate problems, infertility, sexual dysfunction, and sciatica.

Below **The Sphinx represents the spiritual enigma of humanity. It has the body of a beast and the head of a man. As we ascend the human energy system we follow the process of evolution from our animal nature to our spiritual capacity for love, joy, and healing.**

CORRESPONDING DUCTLESS GLANDS AND ORGANS

SOLAR PLEXUS CHAKRA

Ductless gland: **pancreas**

Associated body parts: **stomach, liver, gallbladder, pancreas, small intestine, muscles**

Ailments that arise from imbalance of the Solar Plexus are indigestion, acid stomach, ulcers, hepatitis, gallstones, pancreatitis (inflammation of the pancreas), and diabetes.

HEART CHAKRA

Ductless gland: **thymus**

Associated body parts: **pericardium, heart, lungs, circulation**

Dysfunction of the Heart Chakra can cause arteriosclerosis, angina, myocardial infarction, heart arrhythmia, and stenosis of the heart and lungs. It also affects the lungs with such conditions as pneumonia, chronic bronchitis, and tuberculosis.

THROAT CHAKRA

Ductless gland: **thyroid**

Associated body parts: **throat, mouth, teeth, jaw, ears**

Ailments associated with the Throat Chakra are sore throat, laryngitis, deafness, tooth decay, gum problems, T.M.J. (temporomandibular joint syndrome), and cervical problems of the neck.

BROW CHAKRA

Ductless gland: **pituitary**

Associated body parts: **eyes, sinuses, base of skull, temporal lobes**

The problems associated with a dysfunctional Brow Chakra concern intelligence and stupidity, dull affectivity, and overwork. These problems can create conditions such as migraine, blindness and other eye problems, such as glaucoma and cataracts, brain tumors, and strokes.

CROWN CHAKRA

Ductless gland: **pineal**

Associated body parts: **upper skull, cerebral cortex, skin**

When the Crown Chakra is dysfunctional, there are problems with learning, perception, and spiritual understanding. The physical problems that can occur are epilepsy, color blindness, alcoholism, nervous disorders, neurosis, and insomnia.

unexpressed anger, causes inflammation of the blood. Too much fluid stagnation in the body causes catarrh and excess mucus and can turn into tumors if not reversed.

Our physical bodies are energetic maps. The body has no mind of its own but acts as a mirror for the higher mind, showing us where there is imbalance. We need to read the body as a map of emotional suppression to understand what is going on at a deep level. It shows where there is constriction, or not enough energy in the system.

The body uses energy released from the chakras. If the chakra is congested, energy filtration becomes sluggish. This may be experienced as coldness and lack of vital energy. We may feel tired, out of sorts, or constipated. Too much energy in the chakra appears as heat, irritability, and stagnation.

THE HEALING POWER OF ENERGY

You are advised to consult your physician if you are experiencing any discomfort in these chakra areas. In addition to getting a diagnosis, you may wish to seek out healthy alternatives for relief from your condition. Please refer to the chapter on healing (*see page 110*). It is possible to reduce pain and other physical symptoms without using harsh medical interventions. Sometimes these conditions respond to new ways of thinking about our lives. If you have had a condition for many years, it may be useful to examine your life to see what you were experiencing emotionally at the onset of your physical problems.

If you are sensitive and energetically aware, it is preferable to use alternative medicines rather than to drug the body. The innate healing power of the body is stimulated by energetic treatments. The choice is left to you. Informed choice gives you healthy options for dealing with physical conditions.

Once you have identified the physical complaints you have with the governing chakra, you can use the affirmations and meditations in this book to bring balance and harmony back in alignment with your higher purpose, no matter which type of medicine you choose to use.

The emotions have a profound effect on our healing. They come from our desires and attachments to how we expect our life to be fulfilled. If we are unhappy about a situation, we experience aggression, anxiety, or grief. Whether we are conscious of those feelings and are able to allow them a space in our experience is going to affect energy levels. Suppressing feelings locks them into the subconscious where they congest the energy flow from the chakras.

Aggression that is unexpressed becomes blocked in the musculature of the body. It freezes our muscles and impedes our ability to respond and move. It settles in the back of the neck and behind the throat if we do not say the words that need to be expressed. If we feel like striking out, it can become blocked in our shoulders and upper arms. If anger and frustration stop us from moving forward in our lives, it can become blocked in the calves and thighs.

Reanimating a deadened feeling function can create anxiety because we are not used to the sensation that feelings create. We live in a society that does not allow us to express our feelings easily or comfortably. Yet we need to find appropriate ways of allowing our feelings room in our life. If we swallow our grief and hide our fear, we deny ourselves an opportunity for growth. If we pretend that everything is fine in our life, when it is not, we cut ourselves off from our own aliveness.

Feelings are real but they are not the truth. We are more than our feelings, more than our bodies, and more than our thoughts. However, to deny the life of the body or our emotional reaction cuts us off from energy that can be used for creativity and health. Learning how to manage our emotions comes with practice and maturity.

Emotions ground us in our being and indicate the path to right action. When we know what we are feeling, we can choose appropriate avenues of expression. In the end, emotions are simply energy. How we express that energy is our choice.

VISUALIZING A CHAKRA

A chakra is divided into three sections: the outer lip, the body, and the tip, containing the seeds of our destiny. The outer lip of the chakra acts as a filter to our daily exchanges with our surroundings. If our feelings remain unexpressed, this energy accumulates and congests our energy system. This is what is called energetic dross, and it builds up, causing symptoms of fatigue, aging, and illness.

The main body of the chakra is made up of a fine web of etheric energy. It is composed of the warp and weave of our thoughts and attitudes. If we feel a particular way about something, it will affect how we respond emotionally and, therefore, energetically.

At the very core (or tip) of the chakra is the seed of our destiny. This seed cannot be opened until our negativity and self-limiting ideas have been removed, because they block our energy. Once we begin the inner work of affirming our being and honoring who we are, our destiny begins to unfold. Life changes for us in palpable ways. There are more of the good things we enjoy: more love, more abundance, more awareness.

As we affirm our worth and our choices for health, abundance, and ease, life responds to what we think about ourselves. People who do affirm themselves find that life does become easier and there is enough. Energy follows thought, and, as we open ourselves to what is good and positive, destiny unfolds as it was meant to. Health, joy, prosperity, and well-being emerge out of knowing that we deserve the life we say we want.

We direct our destiny by managing the ways we think. We either become inner-directed, knowing our worth and goodness and experiencing ourselves as enough, or we become outer-directed and dictated to by family pressure and social and religious standards.

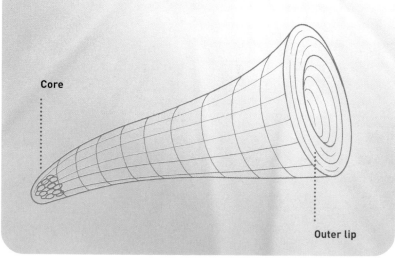

Core

Outer lip

EMOTIONAL EFFECTS

The chakras are extremely responsive to what we think and feel. Unexpressed anger or frustration can accumulate as tension in the muscles. Imploded emotional energy can also overcharge the chakra system, causing imbalance and preventing us from using our energy in a positive way.

THE ROOT CHAKRA

The Root Chakra is affected by aggression, which, if allowed to remain unexpressed, turns into anger and violence. If your life is threatened or your beliefs are attacked, these feelings will surface and stimulate the adrenaline flow into your blood, causing you to become defensive and frightened. Through discovering the emotional charge you have around you, defending your territory, you open reserves of energy you may never have realized you had, which can be used for creativity and a healthy lifestyle.

THE SACRAL CHAKRA

The Sacral Chakra has a less aggressive emotional response. This is the seat of pleasure and well-being. When we are not experiencing these emotions, frustration builds. When feelings emerge, they are often about what we desire or what we lack. This can be for love, sex, money, and joy. Learning to be grateful for what we have releases much of the frustration or sense of loss held in this chakra. We can learn to sublimate this energy into a balanced lifestyle that is focused on a positive emotional expression of what we have and do.

THE SOLAR PLEXUS CHAKRA

The Solar Plexus Chakra's emotions revolve around power. They reflect our relationship to inner strength and self-worth. These emotions help us take a stand for ourselves. If we are comfortable with our power, we will act confidently and exercise freedom of choice in most matters. If we are uncertain and doubtful about our right to our own power, we will evade situations that call for an affirmative response.

THE HEART CHAKRA

The Heart Chakra is the center of love. It opens us to experience love for ourselves and others. It lets us feel compassion, joy, and peace. As the heart expresses love, it permeates all aspects of our life and enriches our relationships. The heart is the essence of joy.

THE THROAT CHAKRA

The Throat Chakra gives expression to our emotions in word and sound. We purr when we are deeply happy, sigh when we are sad, grunt when we are angry, and close our throats down when we are afraid to say what is on our mind. It is the channel for communication and creativity. It is through the throat that we sing our joy, say our prayers for peace, or scream our pain away. Knowing that we have the right to communicate our feelings openly is essential for our life development.

THE BROW CHAKRA

The Brow Chakra regulates our emotional responses. When a situation evokes our feelings, it is through the Brow Chakra that we decide how to respond. If we allow ourselves to feel, emotions can be experienced and disappear. If we suppress our emotions, they revert to the subconscious and block our energy.

THE CROWN CHAKRA

The Crown Chakra has but one emotion and that is bliss. This state is described as a joyful sense of the divine. Once it is experienced, it tends to negate all other emotions. A state of bliss is felt when there is no longer identification with the lower centers. This state of bliss is often called transcendence.

Above **When we harness our vital energy to our willpower we develop the capacity to move with grace, precision, and intent.**

Opposite **A chakra resembles a large cone. The outer lip catches the accumulated stress of the day. The long body is made of the attitudes and ideas we have about life. The seeds of our destiny lie in the very tip of the chakra and cannot be opened until we have harvested out our negativity about life.**

THE CHAKRAS AND THE MENTAL BODY

The ideas and attitudes we have reflect how we were raised: what our families thought about life, what our churches and schools felt was right, and what our culture honored as valuable. We accumulate many self-limiting ideas based on what others perceive to be right. Learning to think for ourselves takes time, many mistakes, and a commitment to life. When we develop wholesome beliefs that reflect a peaceful inner state, our thinking becomes clearer and we become less opinionated about how things should be. The more positive they are, the more resilient our energy system.

ROOT CHAKRA

When our way of life is threatened, the Root Chakra is activated and our ideas become harsh, even hateful in nature. We become defensive and cut off warm feelings to anyone or anything that threatens our home or our institutions. Knowing clearly that we belong in our community and are entitled to preserve our way of life helps us develop tolerance and compassion for strangers and those on the fringe of society.

SACRAL CHAKRA

The Sacral Chakra harbors attitudes about money, health, deservedness, and pleasure. Sexuality has more constraints around it than any other single issue besides money. How people feel about these subjects has a direct result on their personal energy. When we have harsh ideas about pleasure, we will suffer deprivation and, eventually, disease.

SOLAR PLEXUS CHAKRA

The Solar Plexus Chakra holds thoughts about power, confidence, and freedom of choice. If we fail to value ourselves, our ideas about power may be inflated or deflated, depending on how we see ourselves in relation to others. When we know who we are we cultivate power carefully, and cherish our freedom to choose what is right for us.

HEART CHAKRA

The Heart Chakra holds ideas and attitudes about our worthiness to give and receive love. The more we love ourselves and accept the wounds of human fragility, the more we begin to love others. The heart is the seat of joy. We bring healing to the heart when we allow life to be joyful and loving. Learning to place one's love in the sacred vault of another's heart allows the heart to be full. The heart longs to trust in love.

THROAT CHAKRA

The Throat Chakra is controlled by the mind. When we feel comfortable in expressing ourselves, the Throat Chakra is capable of expressing our truth eloquently and with grace. It is in the Throat Chakra that we tune our awareness into the higher mind, which whispers the truth to us through our inner ear. Developing a quiet mind allows us to hear the voice of spirit.

BROW CHAKRA

The Brow Chakra is where our mentality is formulated. It is the control center for the mind. Our intelligence can be used to create harmony or conflict. When we are at one with ourselves, we find we have few thoughts and our mind is still. When we are conflicted, we struggle with our mind, finding the best way to resolve our problems. The Brow Chakra operates holistically. It views life from a more inclusive perspective and points the way to more wholesome choices.

CROWN CHAKRA

The Crown Chakra opens the realm of higher thinking to us. Here we see the entire picture and move beyond the petty details of life. The Crown Chakra is global, even universal, in its approach to situations or people. It has a spiritual dimension that teaches us to consider the origin of conflict, and to see with our heart as well as our head. It is able to put things into perspective.

Above **The Brow Chakra lets us explore the realms of knowledge and develop inner knowing. It stimulates our imagination to envisage the life we say we want.**

Right **Learning new skills is a function of a healthy Brow Chakra. It gives the mind energy to clear a visible path for our life to follow so our gifts and talents can be cultivated.**

Below **Attitudes to sexuality and pleasure are harbored in the Sacral Chakra.**

	PHYSICAL BODY	EMOTIONAL BODY	MENTAL BODY
ROOT CHAKRA	ADRENALS: the fight-or-flight function of the kidneys is activated.	Aggression, anger, violence, jealousy.	Attitudes of separation, exclusivity, territory, belonging, your right to your own space.
SACRAL CHAKRA	OVARIES/TESTES: the reproductive organs, which control sexual development.	Pleasure, feeling good, deservedness, joy/feeling bad, envious, not caring for your physical body.	Attitudes of being and having enough, knowing that you deserve the life you say you want, enjoyment and well-being, delighting in good health, disdain for suffering.
SOLAR PLEXUS CHAKRA	PANCREAS: the organ that processes sugar. It also controls the digestion of food.	Self-worth, confidence, power, clear choices for selfhood.	Attitudes of being well with yourself and knowing your worth, linking into your personal power, which comes from an affirmed sense of selfhood.
HEART CHAKRA	THYMUS: building a strong immunity from pain and disease.	Being capable of love and compassion for self and others.	Attitudes of happiness, joy, and delight, knowing what and who make your heart sing, embracing life.
THROAT CHAKRA	THYROID: controls metabolism and affects physical and mental development.	Releasing feelings through expressing yourself. This includes crying, shouting, laughing, and saying that you are not happy, comfortable, or pleased.	Having a clear sense that expressing your truth is your key to individuality. Speaking the truth, not gossiping, lying, exaggerating.
BROW CHAKRA	PITUITARY: influences metabolism, growth, and other hormones, including those connected with giving birth.	Giving yourself permission to experience your feelings, whatever they are. Choosing when it is appropriate to express how you feel.	Attitudes that are self-confirming, accepting, inclusive. Developing understanding for your own limitations and those of others, cultivating forgiveness and gratitude.
CROWN CHAKRA	PINEAL: produces melatonin and regulates our body clock.	Wanting to cultivate bliss and surrender to what is.	Developing holistic and universal principles of acceptance, respect, and knowing that we never do anything without the help of a higher source.

The SPIRITUAL
dimension

The realm of the spirit opens us to the
all-pervading consciousness of truth,
love, and wisdom. It gives our lives purpose
and teaches us to honor our own inner
guidance for living.

THE POWER OF THOUGHT

The chakras respond in a sensitive and intelligent manner to our thoughts and attitudes. They reflect the nature of our belief system by the levels of energy they filter. We have either an expanded or limited energy field in accordance with those attitudes.

Most of us don't reflect on our basic beliefs, and yet, if we were to look at how we judge ourselves and limit our sense of joy and well-being, we might understand how we also limit our energy. Self-examination can help increase our vitality, health, and happiness.

When attitudes become unbending, the energetic counterpart occurs in the chakras and manifests in our body. If our attitudes are too rigid or too unstructured, our chakras will be exactly the same. Energy follows thought as a river follows its course. If, for instance, we harbor a belief that life is difficult and we should avoid risks, our energy system will show constraint, limitation, and diminished energy flow, particularly in the first three chakras, which hold the unconscious attitudes of family, clan, and community. If we believe that life can prevail and we are willing to take a risk, we will be blessed with the energy we need.

Each chakra has a form of intelligence that allows it to organize energy according to its higher purpose. When we cultivate grounded ideas and wholesome attitudes about ourselves, the chakras perform optimally. They serve as energy conductors to feed our system. Positive awareness opens the portal for energy to flow in the direction of our highest good and greatest joy.

Looking at each chakra's intelligence will show which life issues, qualities, and challenges come under the specific chakras.

We can see what negative attitudes do to constrict energy flow, as well as what positive attitudes do to transform our energetic output.

ROOT CHAKRA

Intelligence: Administrative
Soul lesson: Service

The Root Chakra's intelligence helps us to administer our life force. It is based on order in the energetic economy. It is concerned with the qualities of order, security, structure, and stability that we need to make a viable existence. It encourages attitudes that firmly establish our right to the life we say we want.

If life has been problematic and full of difficulty, it may be important to investigate the attitudes in your family history that reflect mistrust or encourage expectations of insecurity or despair. We need to cultivate attitudes that trust in the goodness of life to us through difficult and challenging times.

The more inner stability we can mentally create, the more grounded life becomes, and the better we are able to cope with change.

SACRAL CHAKRA

Intelligence: Sensation and pleasure
Soul lesson: Peace and wisdom

The Sacral Chakra opens us up to a realm of health, well-being, pleasure, and abundance. If we have attitudes that deny us pleasure, we will live a limited existence. The organism expands with pleasure and contracts with pain. Pleasure helps us sustain a peaceful and joyful life, rich in wisdom about the simple joys of life. The more we develop attitudes that allow us ease, joy, and pleasure, the more energy we have for doing the difficult chores and tasks.

Looking at our attitudes about sensuality, sexuality, ease, abundance, and pleasure helps us mature and become our own person. The more we know ourselves, the

less we are at the mercy of media marketing designed to make us feel we are somehow lacking. When we know what delights us and gives us joy and peace, then buying something to make us feel "good enough" becomes less attractive.

SOLAR PLEXUS CHAKRA

Intelligence: Instinctual knowing
Soul lesson: Human and divine love

The Solar Plexus Chakra quickens when we anchor our personal identity in the abiding nature of the self. This challenges the external labels we use to identify ourselves, which limit who we truly are. If we are identified with being a certain way and we maintain a specific image that people can approve, respect, or accept, we live a life based upon maintaining that image and avoid dealing with our spiritual nature, our true self. Forming wholesome attitudes around selfhood, freedom of choice, personal power, and confidence stems from connecting with our innate sense of worth.

We are value itself, and there is nothing we need do to prove our worth. Once we realize we are worthy, simply because we exist, we free our life force and liberate energy for living.

HEART CHAKRA

Intelligence: Remembering the good
Soul lesson: Brotherhood and Love

The Heart Chakra's attitudes are based on love, compassion, and healing. Developing an open Heart Chakra comes from knowing that we are love itself. As we mature and require less sustenance from the external world to nurture us, we become better able to give out love, warmth, and healing from a

Top left **Instinct is common to all life forms. Our instinctual knowledge is linked to the Solar Plexus. It allows us to be aware of our deep felt, gut reactions to situations and people. Honoring these feelings is both self-protective and necessary for spiritual self-preservation.**

Top right **Teaching opens doors to new realms of awareness where unexpressed potential can be developed. Through knowledge we learn how to negotiate the challenges of life.**

Opposite **Firefighters, police, and soldiers are all in the service of protecting humanity. They help maintain order, structure, and social justice. These are the qualities of the Root Chakra.**

Top **The Heart Chakra is the energy center that unites couples and brings healing to emotional wounds.**

Above **The Crown Chakra is the dominant center for those who bring peace, spiritual teachings, and healing to humanity.**

kind and generous spirit. When we cultivate attitudes based on our right to love and be loved, wounds rooted in anger and loss can be healed. When we are mature we are capable of sustaining love and allowing it to fill our lives. Attitudes rich in love make our life worthwhile because love stays in the heart forever.

The Heart Chakra's need to love is its only driving force. It can be happy loving animals, nature, or the world at large. It thrives on the two-way nature of relationships so that it can function with peace, warmth, care, and a sense of oneness. Allowing the heart to do its job is what the work of the body/mind/spirit continuum is all about.

THROAT CHAKRA

Intelligence: Will and expression
Soul lesson: Expressing divine will

The Throat Chakra's attitudes all nurture a belief in the sanctity of personal expression. This chakra becomes functional when we commit to expressing our truth to the best of our ability. Attitudes about suppressing "negative" feelings, being polite, and not rocking the boat block this chakra and weaken our life force. An essential attitude is that what we say matters, and this belief in self heals this chakra.

If we grew up in a family that put down what we said, then speaking up for ourselves is important to us. Communicating from the depth of our integrity gives us credibility and constancy and defines mature adults who can be trusted and mean what they say.

BROW CHAKRA

Intelligence: Control and wisdom
Soul lesson: Detachment and intuition

The Brow Chakra matures with age and experience. It develops right thinking about who we are and helps us through the difficulties that challenge us. The ability to disengage from attacks, unwholesome situations, or people nurtures our inner clarity and strength. The ability to recognize the nature of people and situations frees us to use our life force appropriately. Healthy attitudes based on love and respect of self and others help us cultivate discernment. This teaches us to make optimal choices based on our highest good and greatest joy. Attitudes rich in flexibility, openness, and a deep love for one's self—and that same beautiful jewel in others—help us manage our lives with grace and wisdom.

CROWN CHAKRA

Intelligence: Spiritual understanding
Soul lesson: To be at one with the source

A healthy Crown Chakra opens us to a spiritual understanding of the oneness of life. It is predicated on the belief that there is no separation at any level in an expanded reality that acknowledges the source of life. We learn that we are always guided and protected. A higher power moves our lives in a caring and loving way. When we connect this understanding with our life experiences, we are able to salvage our spirit through challenging times by seeing how each event opens us to a greater love and connection with spirit.

THE ART OF MEDITATION

Meditation provides a model for you to use when you wish to transform your negative thoughts of unhappiness, hate, or despair. When we find ourselves in unhappy circumstances, or cannot visualize a horizon where we are free from emotional, and sometimes physical, discomfort, it is valuable for us to look within and ask ourselves what we think is the purpose of this situation. What can be trusted? What is permanent? What are we learning about ourselves in the face of difficulties? Sometimes, we get that "Aha!" that tells us we are fine, and life goes on.

It helps us to put our negativity into a broader perspective and see beyond our self-interest. Learning to put our feelings and reactions into a more relative outlook helps us relax and regain our faith and trust in life, even if something has been truly beyond our understanding. It helps us regain hope if we are feeling lost.

Take a moment to reflect on a difficult situation you may presently be in or have recently experienced. These moments are all characterized by unease, tension, fear, doubt, or despair. They bring out the worst, most negative aspect of our personality, where we are disconnected from our higher self, unable to see the light of God's love, and find ourselves falling into despair and fear.

Extricating ourselves from these negative situations can take days, weeks, months, and even years. We are blinded to truth and insight. Feelings of loss, betrayal, separation, and anger can overwhelm us. Yet, in telling the truth about our feelings, we yield to their power and learn about ourselves in the process. We also learn that there is something indelible and permanent that is not affected by emotions. This is the self. The self is the substratum of our existence and it never changes, no matter what is happening on the surface of our lives.

In looking at the situation that has affected you, ask yourself what your feelings are. Do not judge them. Allow them to be a part of your experience. Ask yourself what is permanent. What is the part of you that is not affected by change? What does that feel like?

Now ask yourself if there are any other feelings or thoughts associated with this situation. Did you experience feeling confused, overwhelmed, or distant? Can you allow these feelings to be as they are, real but not the whole truth?

Did you draw conclusions from this situation? Did you resolve anything in experiencing your feelings? Did you become grounded in the reality of your truth? Can you hold your ground with your awareness?

These aspects of looking at any situation can free you from living in denial or chaos about yourself, another person, or a situation. If you trust your feelings and the power of your ability to perceive the truth, you can also make the necessary moves for your health, well-being, and security.

Trust in the source to show you whatever insights you may need to be compassionate, loving, true to yourself, and appropriate with others. Be still and do nothing. Allow the energy you have been holding to be released, and take a moment to be at peace with yourself. Accepting the truth allows you to experience yourself, and this will heal you.

Below **Meditation calms and quiets the mind. It allows our small, edited ego to unite with the higher power of Self, which is always whole, complete, and aware. Through meditation we connect to our spirit and receive guidance to live an ethical and balanced life.**

AFFIRMATIONS FOR THE CHAKRAS

34

The Book of Chakras **The Spiritual Dimension**

This is a practical exercise to let you review some of the negative attitudes associated with each chakra. It illustrates a way of reframing negative attitudes into more positive and life-affirming ones.

ROOT CHAKRA

Negative attitudes: The negative attitudes associated with the Root Chakra have to do with despair and victimhood. These attitudes can generate violent and hateful feelings. These feelings emerge when our life is threatened and we feel overwhelmed. We may experience such thoughts as "It's not worth it"; "I want to die"; "Life is unbearable this way." They all attest to a malignant disassociation from life and a lack of trust in its innate goodness.

Below left **Negative attitudes associated with the Root Chakra include feeling that life is not worth living. Developing a positive attitude is essential.**

Below right **Opening our minds to the beauty and timelessness of nature can bring peace and a sense of unity with the world.**

Affirmations for the Root Chakra

I TRUST IN THE GOODNESS OF LIFE TO CARRY ME THROUGH.
I BELONG WHEREVER I AM.
I CHOOSE LIFE.
I AFFIRM MY RIGHT TO THE LIFE I KNOW I WANT.
I CULTIVATE CONSTANCY, STABILITY, AND A WHOLESOME STRUCTURE TO SUPPORT ME THROUGH LIFE'S CHANGES.
I ACCEPT MYSELF AS I AM.
I AM GRATEFUL FOR THE EXPERIENCES OF MY LIFE.

Positive attitudes: All positive attitudes involving the Root Chakra attest to a spiritual belief in the goodness of life. They imply trust and a sense of belonging, and tell us that there is love, support, and care to get us through difficult and challenging times. It may not come in the form we think we need, but if we are quiet and still we can sense it in nature, in the kindness of strangers, and in many gentle and tender ways. Be still, do nothing. Let the goodness come.

SACRAL CHAKRA

Negative attitudes: The negative attitudes found in the Sacral Chakra tend to be all about our deservedness of a good life. If we feel we are not worthy of feeling good, of having enough of what we need, or of experiencing simple pleasures, we will be unhappy and miserable. We will also make others feel guilty for not making our lives better. Unhealthy attitudes about sexuality and the right to enjoy good health and have abundance will focus on deprivation rather than on our right to what we say we want. These negative attitudes corrode our energy and limit our life force. They instill strict and pious attitudes while serving to cut us off from ease, joy, and pleasure.

Affirmations for the Sacral Chakra

I ALLOW PLEASURE AND GOODNESS INTO MY LIFE.
I KNOW THAT I DESERVE GOODNESS AND JOY.
I ACCEPT THAT GOOD HEALTH IS MY NATURAL STATE.
I ALLOW ABUNDANCE INTO MY EXPERIENCE.
I OPEN MYSELF TO SIMPLE, HEALING PLEASURES.
I CULTIVATE HEALTH, WHOLENESS, AND EASE.
I DESERVE TO FEEL PEACE IN MY LIFE.

Below **The Sacral Chakra benefits when we respect our health and well-being. Nurturing the physical body helps us develop positive attitudes about our deservedness.**

Positive attitudes: Developing a wholesome outlook toward our body by respecting its need for rest, recreation, touch, and expression helps us transform negative attitudes into healthy ones. Finding the balance between work and ease, prosperity and charity, pushing the body and giving it rest teaches us about wholesome limits. Nurturing the body with tenderness and care creates an attitude that we are deserving. It creates a possibility for ease and strengthens our right to pleasure.

SOLAR PLEXUS CHAKRA

Negative attitudes: Any time we deny our essential worth, we give away our power and deplete this chakra. The foundation of the Solar Plexus Chakra is an acceptance of our intrinsic value as a person with individual rights. These concern respect for and the worth of our being. Whether or not things are going well does not affect our sense of worth. It is not negotiable, nor is it determined by external events. Negative attitudes that deny our selfhood deprive us of love, kindness, and respect. They diminish us by letting us be manipulated and exploited.

Positive attitudes: Honoring the self allows a wealth of respect, kindness, and goodness to come our way. When we acknowledge the wealth of our being, we will seek out situations and people who honor us as individuals and affirm our worth. When we value ourselves, others will have no choice but to do the same and treat us with kindness and respect. When we say yes to who we are, people will either drop out of our lives or act respectfully. Cultivating a sense of worth may feel unfamiliar at first. Begin by making small, incremental shifts in how you perceive yourself. Give this time to grow and develop. Allow the truth of your experience to keep you balanced so that you become neither inflated and bigger than you really are nor deflated, unworthy, and undervalued.

Affirmations for the Solar Plexus Chakra

I KNOW THAT WHO I AM IS LOVE, INTELLIGENCE, AND GOODNESS.
I AM WORTHY OF A GOOD LIFE.
I AM CONFIDENT THAT LIFE WILL SUPPORT ME THROUGH ALL ITS CHANGES.
I USE MY POWER WISELY.
I CHOOSE LIFE, LOVE, AND GOODNESS.
I AM IN TOUCH WITH THE SOURCE OF MY POWER.
I AM A RADIANT AND WHOLE BEING, ABLE TO FIND MY PATH IN LIFE.

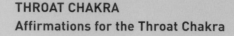

HEART CHAKRA

Negative attitudes: The fear of giving and receiving love blocks health, joy, and goodness from coming into our lives. Fear is the opposite of love. It prevents the heart from being happy and joyful and corrodes the spirit. Avoiding doing what delights us and suffering over loss weakens the heart. Failing to do what we love deprives the heart of its main purpose, which is to love.

Positive attitudes: Allowing love to be the core of our life carries us through difficult and challenging times. It keeps our spirit open and our heart alive. Loving who we are, what we do, and how things are raises the spirit and heals the heart. Knowing that we are love is part of the very fiber of our being. It helps us create a positive, generous attitude toward others and heals wounds of pain, loss, or separation. Love is the greatest gift we can give ourselves. It makes us whole.

Affirmations for the Heart Chakra

I LOVE TO BE LOVED.
I AM LOVE.
LOVE IS AT THE CENTER OF MY LIFE.
LOVE HEALS ME AND MAKES ME NEW.
LOVE IS ALL THAT TRULY MATTERS IN LIFE.
LOVE CONNECTS ME TO THE INFINITE AND MAKES ME WHOLE.
LOVE RESTORES MY FAITH IN LIFE.

Below **Allowing ourselves to be open to love and friendship is essential for the health of the Heart Chakra.**

THROAT CHAKRA

Affirmations for the Throat Chakra

I SPEAK MY TRUTH AND HONOR MY COMMITMENT TO IT.
I EXPRESS MYSELF AS HONESTLY AS I CAN.
I SHARE MY FEELINGS WITH EASE AND COMFORT.
I LIVE FROM MY INTEGRITY.
I COMMUNICATE WHAT IS SO FOR ME, WITHOUT PROJECTING MY TRUTH ONTO OTHERS.
I EXPRESS MYSELF AS CREATIVELY AS POSSIBLE.
I LISTEN TO MY INNER TRUTH.

Negative attitudes: The fear of expressing our truth blocks and limits our energy. If we feel that we have no right to speak out or that no one wants to listen to us, we dampen our life force and negate the precious gift of communication. Lying, substance abuse, and gossip are three things that damage the precious fiber of the Throat Chakra. All of them take us away from our natural goodness and numb us to truth. Feeling we can say things without following through with congruent actions demeans our personal integrity. When we lie, gossip, or trash our bodies with drugs, we lose credibility and respect.

Positive attitudes: Honoring the truth and communicating it from a place of integrity is what makes us responsible adults. When we know we have something to say and it is worth expressing, we make a difference. We expand the Throat Chakra and open our energy field when we share our truth. We learn that both our personal truth and the higher truth of God are sacred. Also, learning appropriate times and ways to express our truth is worth the effort because others can then respond to us.

BROW CHAKRA

Negative attitudes: All negative ideas stem from the one belief that we are not enough. We are not lovable or worthy of having the life we say we want. When we identify with a lack of worth, we fail to honor our true light. Being forever cynical, anxious, and negative makes us ugly and old. Being inflated, separated from our true self, leads to egotism and narcissism. These attitudes develop when we feel we are not "enough" and need to be "more" in the eyes of others. Self-importance limits our truth as well as our vitality.

Positive attitudes: The quintessential belief that we are worthy of receiving our good makes the mind healthy and whole. Accepting the best of ourselves helps us form clearly defined boundaries so that an attack cannot diminish us. Acknowledging our worth lets us know who and what are for our highest good. Loving ourselves lets us cultivate a sense of humor and makes our path through life more joyful. It also opens up our energy field.

Affirmations for the Brow Chakra

MY LOVE OF LIFE REFLECTS ITSELF IN
ALL THAT I SEE AND DO.
I ACKNOWLEDGE MY WORTH AND
ACCEPT MY GOODNESS.
MY NATURE IS WHOLE.
I AM ABLE TO DISCERN THE GOOD
FROM WHAT PULLS MY SPIRIT DOWN.
I FIND WISDOM FROM MY PAST AND
HEALING IN THE PRESENT.
I USE MY INTELLIGENCE AND
INTUITION TO LIGHT MY WAY
FORWARD.
I CULTIVATE A POSITIVE OUTLOOK IN
ALL SITUATIONS.

CROWN CHAKRA

Negative attitudes: The most egotistical belief is that we are doing it all alone. This belief fortifies the ego and gives it license to exploit and manipulate. We thus fail to recognize a higher power than our limited self. This attitude fosters arrogance, false pride, and an over-inflated ego that lives under the pretence that it is invincible and unconquerable, concepts that are both untrue and unhealthy. It separates a person from contact with humanity and keeps the heart closed to love and healing.

Affirmations for the Crown Chakra

I ACKNOWLEDGE THE PRESENCE OF
SPIRIT WORKING IN MY LIFE.
I SEE THE ONE TRUE REALITY.
GOD WORKS IN MY LIFE REGARDLESS
OF MY LIMITATIONS.
I AM OPEN TO THE HEALING POWER
OF SPIRIT WORKING IN MY LIFE.
THE DIVINE GUIDES ME ON THE
PATH OF LIFE.
I RELEASE FEAR, DOUBT, AND PAIN AS I
ACCEPT THAT MY LIFE IS BLESSED.
I SURRENDER MY ARROGANCE AND
EGO TO A HIGHER POWER THAN
MYSELF.

Positive attitudes: Healthy Crown Chakra attitudes embrace a sense of gratitude for one's life and humility for goodness received and experienced. When we realize God loves, protects, and guides us, we anchor our consciousness in a different reality based on faith rather than anxiety. Our everyday, mundane life becomes infused with spirit and grace, and we let go of the small and petty irritations that cause us distress. Spiritual awareness deepens our life, giving it meaning and a sense of higher purpose.

Left Vanity is a negative attitude of the Brow Chakra. When we feel we need to be different in the eyes of others, we are saying that we are not lovable or worthy, and we fail to honor our true self.

Above Arrogance, pride, and egotism are negative attitudes of the Crown Chakra. Feelings of humility and gratitude open our hearts to love and healing.

DECODING YOUR *chakras*

When you learn that you can master your own energy field, you find a level of empowerment and vitality that enables you to find and fulfill your life purpose. Understanding your energy system is the first tool to healing what may be out of balance or deficient in your life.

THE ROOT CHAKRA
MULADHARA
Root or support

The Root Chakra is concerned with keeping life vibrant and sustainable. It incorporates all the qualities to maintain existence in an orderly fashion, including being constant and stable. It is drawn to the simple activity of staying alive. It focuses upon shelter and sustenance, as well as the things that keep our lives moving along. It flourishes with levels of security that keep chaos and evil far from our door, and ultimately it is concerned with having the patience and presence to see our dreams come true.

The symbol of the Root Chakra

Root Chakra

QUALITIES AND ATTRIBUTES

Building a structure that supports and sustains our life is a function of the Root Chakra. If our structures are not stable enough to support us we may become unsure about our right to what we want. Cultivating stability while we form the structure of our life helps us to handle change.

Security is an aspect of the Root Chakra that helps to keep us focused and grounded. When we don't feel secure we lose energy, fearing for our existence and wondering whether we will go on. Cultivating a deep sense of inner security helps keep the Root Chakra functional during uncertainty.

The Root Chakra carries all the qualities of survival from our ancestors. If our people fought to maintain a way of life or to find a better life, their courage and tenacity are part of our genetic heritage. Just as the roots of diseases are transmitted down family lines, so are the spiritual qualities. When we find ourselves in difficult circumstances, we can draw on the qualities our ancestors possessed to see them through. We can tap into courage, cunning, stealth, and a ruthless desire to live. It is in our Root Chakras.

The Root Chakra controls the fight-or-flight reaction that triggers the adrenal cortex. This function stimulates the flow of adrenaline into the blood when we are under attack, putting us into survival mode.

The Root Chakra anchors itself to the earth when we are patient, resourceful, and hopeful about our lives. Remaining positive and open to possibilities strengthens the Root Chakra and allows for stability and inner strength. Anchoring our spirit in reality is the quintessential quality of this chakra.

Location: In the perineum at the base of the spine

Age of resonance: Conception to 7

Shape: Large cube

Glandular connection: Cortex of the adrenal gland (on the upper end of each kidney in humans), which secretes a number of steroid hormones, including the corticosteroids cortisol and corticosterone

Color: Red

Musical note: C

Type of music: Drumming

Element: Earth

Aspect of intelligence: Administrative

Sensory experience: Smell

Essential oils: Cinnamon, garlic, sandalwood

Crystals: Ruby, bloodstone, hematite

Aspects of the solar system: Earth, Saturn

Astrological association: Capricorn

Metal: Lead

Earthly Location: The Indian preserves and their sacred lands. The sacred lands of all indigenous people

Mythological animal: White elephant with seven trunks

Plant: Sage

Qualities: Patience, structure, stability, security, the ability to manifest your dreams

Life issues: To value the material as sacred, to find trust in place of despair, to persevere

Physical activities: Yoga, movement of any kind that activates the legs and feet. Any form of activity that is grounding, physical, and demands presence

Spiritual activities: Noticing the beauty and perfection of the natural world

Positive archetype: Mother

Negative archetype: Victim

Angelic presence: Archangel Michael, leader of the heavenly armies against the forces of evil

ARCHETYPES

POSITIVE: The Mother

The Mother is a person, either male or female, who is nurturing, positive, and hopeful. Mothers encourage, acknowledge, and affirm our being through love, kindness, and absolute faith in the goodness of life. They make the dark moments bearable because they bring us hope of a positive outcome.

NEGATIVE: The Victim

The victim is a person who, because of external circumstances, is unable to rally regenerative forces and go forward in life. Victims stay alive through the grace and generosity of other agencies and have little chance of renewing their connection with life as long as they remain dependent upon others to maintain life. They may be temporarily invalided, victims of terrifying circumstances, or completely uprooted from a life they have previously enjoyed.

THE INFLUENCE OF THE ROOT CHAKRA

We all face times in life that challenge our resources and try our patience. Few people are taught to be internally resourceful when things go wrong. Developing our resources comes from living life and experiencing change. A healthy Root Chakra is buoyant and flexible. It is adaptable and can remain grounded through changes.

When people become uprooted from their homes and are forced through circumstances to move elsewhere, they will seek a similar condition to the one they know. Imagine a tree that has grown in a certain climate, in specific soil, with fixed amounts of sun, water, and wind. If you uprooted this tree and tried to plant it elsewhere, out of its adaptability zone, it would fail to thrive or would die. People

THE ROOT CHAKRA AND THE ADRENAL CORTEX

The cortex is the outer portion of the adrenal gland (the inner portion is called the medulla). The cortex produces corticosteroids, which maintain balanced levels of acidity and alkalinity in the cells. It releases amino acids, promotes liver glycogen and glucose formation, and monitors cardiac activity and blood pressure. It controls the flow of adrenaline, which fuels our fight-or-flight responses to accidents, stresses, or threats. The adrenaline response can save our lives and keep us actively present in any life-threatening situation. The kidneys themselves contain ancestral vitality and life force. We are dependent on their healthy function to stay anchored in life.

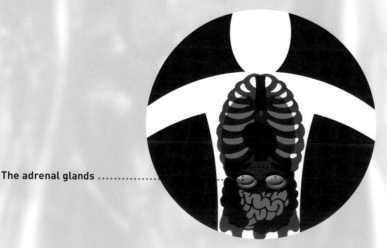

The adrenal glands ....

are the same. They need optimal conditions to make successful changes in themselves or their environment.

Even though we are an adaptable and mobile culture when crisis hits, we revert to our basic instincts for survival. Our thoughts turn to shelter, food, water, and warmth. These are fundamental to our lives and come before the realm of comfort, power, love, or ideas.

People during times of crisis seek community. They bond with others and reach out in ways previously unknown before they were threatened. Tribal and clan ties sustain people in times of change, and help stabilize the Root Chakra.

During normal times we are able to turn our attention to developing other qualities. When we find ourselves in new situations under different circumstances, our Root Chakra becomes destabilized and we struggle to maintain both inner and outer equilibrium. At these times it takes only the slightest upset to send us plummeting into despair.

Finding a steady and permanent connection with what is real and true can sustain us through change. Knowing the highest and most eternal truths about the Source can sustain us when our grounding is weak and our spirit diminished. Creating a spiritual context in which to place our life experiences is emotionally sustaining.

The Root Chakra contains within its structure the underlying attitudes we have about the nature of life. If our ancestors struggled and found life perilous, we will inherit an underlying belief that life is hard and we must struggle. As the Root Chakra is affected by war, pestilence, famine, and chaos, all human beings have some level of dysfunction in their Root Chakras. Few people are truly grounded in a positive and loving sense of life.

All of us have been either uprooted or affected by the hardships of life—if not directly then through our family history. What our ancestors and family members experienced during hard times is a genetic memory we carry within us. Each time we are stressed or feel threatened we will react from that place within us where we fear the worst, doubt our chances for survival, and feel that we do not have a right to the life we say we want.

When we realize that the past has no hold over us, we are free to make our own interpretation of the events in our lives. We are encouraged to try harder, to take a stand for ourselves, and persevere. If the Root Chakra carries too many constrictions and dictates how we feel life needs to be, then we will be pulled down by the weight of tradition, family values, and religious precepts, which will limit and prescribe how we think things need to be. This is neither adaptable nor essential.

We are far more than our family upbringing, our schooling, or our religious beliefs. We are more than our physical body, our emotional stability, and our mental framework about what we think life is. When we expand our consciousness to include the substratum upon which life is based, which is a spiritual consciousness that is eternal, we can be unruffled by the changing tide of events that affect us.

When people live exclusively within the Root Chakra, they are overly attached to land, tradition, home and family, and clan or tribal roots. They do not find their unique individuality or come to express their talents outside the context of these perimeters.

When people exist entirely from their Root Chakras, they are aware only of the petty differences that divide people and nations. They fail to see the bigger picture of one people, one planet. Part of healing the Root Chakra is to eliminate a sense of difference. We open the Root to be an anchor for our spirit and to manifest unity rather than separation.

The archetype of the Root Chakra is the Mother. She feeds, nourishes, and provides for our needs. When we honor her we honor ourselves. Loving and taking care of ourselves is how we become our own good mother. Learning to listen and trust our needs and paying attention to what is good, wholesome, and nourishing for us keeps us grounded. This helps release the negative from our lives and live simply, honestly, and with integrity. Healing our roots is learning that we can do more than our parents did and be more than they were able to be. We broaden our scope and expand our possibilities so that life grows rather than narrows. In essence, we become the best we can be by developing the inner qualities that the Root Chakra stands for so that we can adapt, make changes, and live creatively.

Opposite **It is said that the origins of humanity can be traced to one African woman. This fecund, female energy anchors us deep into the roots of the earth, herself the Great Mother who sustains us.**

Below **The barn is a symbol of fertility and prosperity, organization and cultivation. It represents structure, stability, and security, as well as a dream manifested. These are all qualities of the Root Chakra.**

HOW TO ACCESS THE ROOT CHAKRA

We can develop viable and healthy Root Chakras when we affirm our right to a good life. This comes when we honor who we are, beyond any limiting identifications that define us by race, age, religion, or nationality. This way it is easy to say yes to life. When we have strong roots we affirm our right to be present, as well as making choices for our health and well-being. As we affirm ourselves, we strengthen our attachment to life and open the space for it to be fulfilled through us.

Each time we define ourselves by the self-limiting ideas that dictate where we can and cannot go, whom we can or cannot participate with, and what we are allowed to do and not do, we narrow our life choices. We define ourselves through race, religion, culture, age, gender, and sexual orientation. We heal our Root Chakra by making choices for ourselves based on the artful attraction, and the promise of growth, maturation, and spiritual development.

A tight and constricted Root Chakra can be filled with hatred, prejudice, and petty attitudes that dictate what we can and cannot do. Cultures that limit the full

AFFIRMATIONS FOR THE ROOT CHAKRA

Repeat these affirmations once every morning and once every evening when you wish to connect with the Root Chakra.

I LIVE FROM MY INTEGRITY

I LOVE FROM MY HEART. I AM CONNECTED TO LIFE IN ALL ITS GLORY.

I know who I am and make choices based on what I know to be right for me.
I affirm my right to the life I choose.
I confirm my right to belong and be a part of something greater than myself.
I know I am truly good.
I live from the depths of my soul longing to express itself in the world.
I stand for justice, truth, and love.
I am supported in life through all my choices to do good and share the light of love.
My body supports me in living a creative and happy life.
I am open to the spirit of life, which carries me beyond my original limits to a higher, more creative space.
I am thankful for all the opportunities for growth and development that have come my way.
I am grateful for the challenges that have taught me who I truly am.
I love life.

expression and creativity of their members based on traditional beliefs have narrow and inflexible Root Chakras.

We may cherish the simplicity of Third World culture and primitive societies. They maintain their integrity by strictly defining who has power and who does not, who can do certain things and who cannot. We may admire the fact that their practices are ancient and their bond to family and clan keep their culture intact. This culture is maintained at the sacrifice of the individual. Talents, gifts, and solutions to community problems are sacrificed because of inflexibility and prejudice.

Our Root Chakra, in order to be functional, must be rid of narrow beliefs. When we have a clear understanding that

Opposite **Ancient myth says that man was fashioned from clay from the earth, into which God breathed life. Our links to the earth keep our lives simple, creative, and productive.**

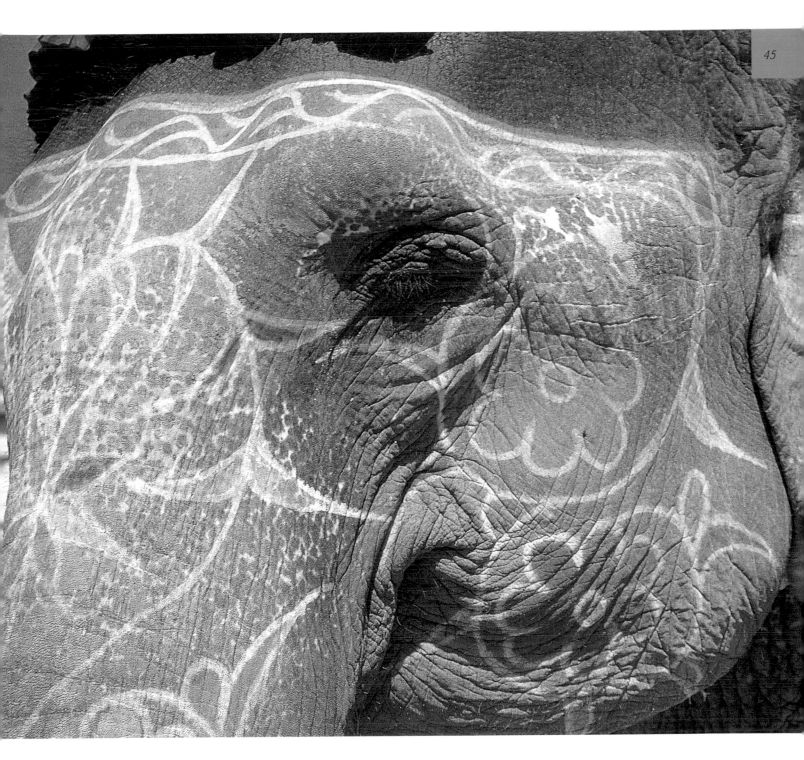

Above **The elephant is the mythical animal for the Root Chakra. In India he is called Ganesh, bringer of good fortune, happiness, and health.**

the Source exists within each and every one of us, we are more open to what unites us than what separates us. We heal the Root Chakra each time we affirm our right to the life we say we want. Knowing we have a right to joy, happiness, health, and a creative existence is fundamental to life. You need no one's approval, nor do you need reasons to make the choices that promise you happiness, stability, and joy. Stepping away from the prescribed dictates of family, culture, or religion may be painful at first, but eventually your roots become defined by the way you live, love, and communicate, and the choices you make for your life.

MEDITATION FOR THE ROOT CHAKRA

Take a few moments to reflect on your early childhood. Can you visualize the home you grew up in and the people who were around you in your early childhood? Take some time to remember what you were like as a child. Can you identify qualities you possess now that you had then? Can you see traces of your nature reflected in who you are now?

Ask yourself the truth about your past and see if you can see a logical pattern that emerged to make you the person you are today. What qualities do you cherish about yourself today that are different than the child who grew up in your early childhood home? Are you more resolute, and better equipped to deal with situations and understand life in a more philosophical way? If you could offer any guidance to the child that you were, what would that be? Hold this child in your heart and bless it for knowing, instinctively, what to do to become the person you are today.

VISUALIZE a large RED CUBE at the very base of your SPINE...

When you have done this, take several deep breaths as though into the seat of your pants. Visualize your breath penetrating to the base of your spine. Each time you inhale, feel the air you drew in energize your life force and anchor you in your legs and feet. Feel your feet connected to the ground. Visualize a large red cube at the very base of your spine. Expand the form and intensify the color. Feel the weight of this large red cube anchoring you to the earth. Feel you are cultivating the qualities of patience, stability, structure, and security in your life. You are creating a space for your dreams to manifest as you develop a realistic approach to living. Feel you can administer order in your life and find solutions to the problems you may be experiencing. You have all the inner resources you need to make your life work and the maturity, stamina, and perseverance to see your dreams turn into reality.

Is there a dream that you would like to see realized? Can you see yourself experiencing the reality of this dream? Allow feelings of fulfillment to expand your energy field as you bring your awareness down to the base of your spine. Once again, expand the form of the Root Chakra and intensify the color red. Say yes to your dreams. Feel the energy from this large red cube move down your legs, through your feet, and into the ground.

Know that with patience, stability, and a sense of security your dream can come true. Affirm your right to life. Say yes to all the trials and tribulations that have brought you to this place of sensitivity and awareness. As difficult as your road may be, aren't you grateful for the inner qualities you have developed, the grit it took to achieve the things you truly wanted? Acknowledge the gifts of courage, stamina, and perseverance that you have accessed from your roots. Native Americans always say, "Thanks to the ancestors." They know we grow on the deeds that came before us and that the next generation will grow from what we do today.

Now seal the Root Chakra with a cross of light within a circle of light. Expand the light to include your entire body, the room you are in, the town and country you live in, and the planet itself. Know you are always part of a greater whole and that who you are makes a difference. Take a deep breath as you affirm your being.

CRYSTALS

RUBY

This precious stone contains the essence of vitality and the regenerative forces. A handful of this stone strengthens and revives the heart. It represents the life force in all its power and is valued for its beauty, fire, and sense of spirit.

BLOODSTONE

This stone is a bright orange-red. It is said to possess the ability to purify the blood. It has a large magnetic field, which is believed to heal physical problems, especially those where the blood is stagnant or impure.

HEMATITE

This is a form of magnetic ore with high density. Its silver color attracts the eye and its magnetic qualities make it good for grounding the spirit. Carrying the stone in one's pocket can help keep one's consciousness focused and grounded.

QUESTIONNAIRE ON THE ROOT CHAKRA

The questions for the Root Chakra focus on stability, structure, patience, and security. If you are weak in any particular area, cultivate patience and inwardly create these qualities over a period of time. They can be attained through your conscious awareness of their importance in your life.

Patience

- Are you a patient person?
- Do you know how to let things come around in your favor over time?
- Can you wait for your projects to manifest by staying focused?
- Are you addicted to fast fixes and immediate results?
- Are you aware that your impatience is sapping your life energy and burning precious fuel needed for your health and well-being?
- To what degree can you connect your impatience with not being fully present for yourself?
- Is impatience or patience a family characteristic?
- Where do your courage, stamina, and grit come from?

- Can you identify family members who were known to have the ability to withstand hardship and change?

- What qualities would you like to develop to help you be more patient with yourself and others?

Structure

- Do you create a life that supports your being the best you can be?
- Do you find fulfillment in the life you have created for yourself?
- To what degree do you need to amend the structures that support your life?
- Can you reflect on a time in your life when you felt supported and upheld?
- Can you internalize that support and make it part of the structure of your life?
- What qualities do you need to cultivate in order to build the life you say you want?
  - Can you be realistic about the levels of support you need to manage your life?
  - Are you building permanent structures that can help you over the difficult moments in life?
  - What do you feel is missing in your support system?
  - How would you transform this?

Stability

- How stable do you feel your life is at this moment?
- Are you in need of cultivating higher degrees of internal stability to see you through up-and-coming changes?
- How would you go about creating more stability in your life?

- Is there something that needs to be transformed for this to happen?
- How would you visualize stability? Does it have a feeling or a picture to it?
- What do you define as stability for yourself?
- Can you recall feeling stable in the past?
- Is stability a quality you are familiar with in your history?
- Do you want to cultivate stability in order to realize your dreams about life?
- Being stable means being consistent with your choices for good. Do you bring this into your life?

Security

- How secure do you feel about your life?
- Do you have the basics covered such as shelter, food, water, and the ability to obtain what you need in times of crisis?
- Do you feel that your life is grounded in reality or are you disconnected from yourself?
- Do you have a sense of direction about what would give you fulfillment and peace of mind?
- Can you resonate with your highest good and trust that you will be secure when you do what fulfills your spirit?
- Are you internally secure in life and able to withstand changes readily?
- Can you create a sense of security for yourself by knowing that you will be all right no matter what happens around you?
- Can you trust that you are protected and guided as you make your way through life?
- Are you fearful of what exists outside your boundaries?

- Are you prejudiced about those who do not live their lives as you do?

Manifestation

- Do you allow yourself to dream of the life you say you want?
- Are there things and experiences you would like to manifest for you?
- Do you trust that your highest good and greatest joy are possible for you?
- Do you feel that you need to change anything in your life for your dreams to come true?
- Do you feel that you are deserving of what you say you want?
- Can you be patient and let your dreams come to fulfillment?
- Can you remain directed doing whatever needs to be done, to realize your intentions?
- Can you integrate your dreams into your present life so that they are part of what you do for yourself each day?
- Are you grateful for the things you have in life now?
- Do you appreciate the dreams that have come true for you in the past?

Left **The Root Chakra is governed by the planet Saturn, which rules time, change, and stability. Learning to develop patience, cultivate stability, and develop structure bring security and the manifestation of our dreams and desires.**

THE COLOR OF
THE ROOT CHAKRA: RED

Red is the color of the life force. It represents courage, passion, anger, and even violence. It is the color that represents earth energy, anchoring us to the planet that sustains us. It is the most visible color in the entire spectrum and has been used traditionally to signify danger, poison, or threat. The color pulls the retina forward so that our energy is engaged outside of ourselves. It warms, heats, and tones our blood. Too much red can raise blood pressure and create irritation.

WORKING THROUGH NEGATIVITY

- Cultivate patience so that when things do not go as planned you do not lose energy by being angry or frustrated.
- Allow time for things to come around in a positive way for you. If you do not succeed in the beginning of a project, rethink it and let things develop in the light of positive affirmation. They will do so eventually, if you can persevere.
- Do what is necessary to remain stable through change. Develop meditation skills and ways to slow down the mind. Learn to be philosophical when things become uncertain.
- Learn to live with change. Be flexible and adaptable.
- Be secure in yourself and know that everything will be all right eventually.
- Trust in life to see you through the difficult moments.
- Do not despair when things do not go well for you. Breathe, give yourself time to reflect on what is essential and important.
- Make a plan to see your dreams unfold. Life without a dream is dull.
- Be grateful for the life you have and work to bring as much order into your life as possible so that when things do go astray you have some reserves to fall back on.
- Enjoy life and cultivate a sense of humor. We all have setbacks and challenges. We are all learning to be resourceful and to cultivate a positive outlook.

THE SACRAL CHAKRA
SVADHISTHANA
My own sweet abode

The Sacral Chakra controls our physical health and well-being. It is the chakra that focuses the life force into building a strong and viable immune system, and keeping the physical body functional and active. It controls our motion and our emotion, and is ruled by the water element, which is directly influenced by how we experience our emotions. When we retain our feelings, water is also retained in the body. This creates bloating and puffiness, a condition known as idiopathic edema.

The symbol of the Sacral Chakra

Sacral Chakra

QUALITIES AND ATTRIBUTES

The essence of the Sacral Chakra is knowing that what we have and do is good enough. This is the center of physical procreation and the chakra directly affecting sexual maturation. It controls our appetites for food, sex, and pleasure. If we are too indulgent we burn up vital life fuel required by other systems in our body. If we hold back too much energy from the physical part of our lives, we become hungry for what we deny ourselves. Finding the balance between control and letting go is essential for this chakra to function.

The Sacral Chakra is concerned with our physical well-being. This means that we learn to honor the body by giving it what it needs to thrive—nutritious food, plenty of rest, and fun, work, and exercise.

This chakra is also concerned with the quality of deservedness. When we feel that we truly deserve the good we long for, we treat ourselves well. We give ourselves permission to have the things we want.

Pleasure is another quality of the Sacral Chakra. It concerns our ability to receive and allow more pleasure into our lives. When we make our lives complex, we strip away the pleasure from our experiences. Finding what is simple can generate joy and pleasure, which nourish the Sacral Chaka.

It takes discipline and maturity to balance this chakra. Abusing our life force depletes our vital energy and leaves us open to disease and emotional unbalance.

A healthy Sacral Chakra has defined limits that are neither too open nor too closed. Respecting these limits nourishes the life of the body and lets us know that we are enough for ourselves.

Location: Two inches below the navel and two inches into the pelvis

Age of resonance: 7–14

Shape: Pyramid

Glandular connection: Ovaries/testes

Color: Orange

Musical note: D

Type of music: Latin dance

Element: Water

Aspect of intelligence: Sensation/pleasure

Sensory experience: Taste

Essential oils: Jasmine, neroli, orange blossom

Crystals: Carnelian, tiger's eye, onyx

Aspect of the solar system: Jupiter

Astrological associations: Cancer, Scorpio

Metal: Tin

Earthly location: Brazil

Mythological animal: A hungry sea monster, waiting to be fed

Plant: Jasmine

Qualities: Well-being, sexuality, sensuality, pleasure, abundance

Life issues: To know that who you are and what you do are enough; to have enough rest, food, exercise, fun, and money; not to link self-worth with what you do or have; to create healthy boundaries to protect your vital life force.

Physical activities: Yoga, dance, swimming, walking

Spiritual activities: Meditation, celibacy, fasting

Positive archetype: Emperor/Empress

Negative archetype: Martyr

Angelic presence: Archangel Metatron

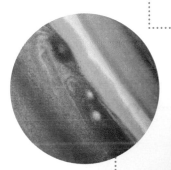

ARCHETYPES

POSITIVE: The Emperor/Empress
The Emperor or Empress is a person who enjoys and respects the physical world. Emperors and Empresses love to have abundance, well-being, and a high degree of pleasure. They know they deserve to feel good about life and enjoy good food, comfort, and some luxury. They are not necessarily spiritual by nature but they do feel at home on the physical plane and enjoy the good life.

NEGATIVE: The Martyr
Martyrs deprive themselves of the simple physical pleasures of life. At some basic level, they feel cheated of the goodness of life and punish themselves by forbidding themselves the warmth and comfort they long for. They are full of guilt and project this onto others, making them suffer too.

THE INFLUENCE OF THE SACRAL CHAKRA

This chakra embodies the totality of our physical health and emotional well-being. It can bring us the highest degree of health or be the most dysfunctional of all energy centers in the human energy system. When people abuse their bodies, treating them like machines that need only to be fueled and rested occasionally, they fail to realize that the body is a vessel for the spirit. The Sacral Chakra works from a deep unconscious realm where our attitudes about ourselves create our physical well-being. Our relationship to health, well-being, and joy reflects how much we value ourselves and honor our spirit on the physical plane.

The function of this chakra depends on how well we take care of ourselves and know our boundaries and limitations. Proper function insures that we harness our life force so that we can be creative and spiritual. This chakra promotes regeneration by feeding vital energy into our systems. It stimulates hormonal flow and influences our motility. It controls the way we move and our desire to exercise.

We preserve our energy and health by forming wholesome attitudes about optimal health. We need energy, not only for daily

THE SACRAL CHAKRA AND THE REPRODUCTIVE GLANDS

The reproductive glands are the ovaries in women, testes in men; they are governed by the Sacral Chakra and develop by the age the chakra is fully formed at around 14. Their function is to reproduce life and keep the species alive. They develop according to our attitudes about growing into adulthood and being responsible for our sexuality. Problems in this area have a matching counterpart corresponding to our attitudes about sexuality. They are influenced by our relationship to our bodies and how we value our spiritual as well as animal nature. Problems in physical maturation and reproduction are connected to these glands, as well as our attitudes about growing up, having a family, and enjoying our sexuality.

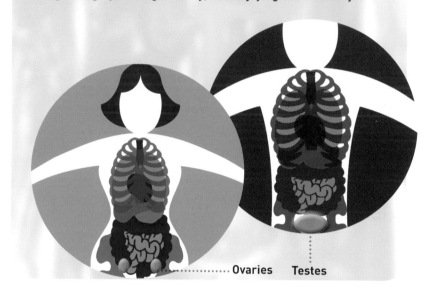

Ovaries   Testes

Left **Money is a symbol of abundance and prosperity in our lives. When we heal the Sacral Chakra we know we have enough and that our cups are half full and not half empty.**

tasks and to enjoy pleasure, but also to protect us through times of challenge and stress. The body, like our bank account, needs to be replenished from time to time, so that we can draw on the goodness that is within it.

Finding the right lifestyle, one that encourages physical regeneration, keeps the Sacral Chakra active. Good nutrition is medicine for the body. Keeping the body hydrated and giving it ample rest and time off from stress and pressure keep us stable and happy. Difficult and challenging experiences strip our bodies of vital energy and deplete our reserves. If this chakra is not replenished it will drain all other chakras to fill it and, eventually, deplete the entire energy resources of the body.

Appreciating the physicality of the body without becoming compulsive or obsessional conserves energy and creates health. It fills the seas of energy reserves that the system can draw from in stressful times. We create these reserves each time we do something good for the body such as oxygenating our blood with exercise, taking time to smell the roses, and relaxing. Each time we feel good about ourselves and honor our choices, we contribute to our physical presence.

The underlying theme of the Sacral Chakra is knowing what is enough. This includes the food we put into our bodies, as well as what we do with our vital energy. Do you dissipate it by giving it away to people and situations that are not pleasurable? Knowing what you do with your physical energy on a daily basis can help you understand what you need for health and well-being. Looking at where you give your energy away can help you make some choices about replenishing it.

Recuperating from illness or abusive situations requires regenerating the Sacral Chakra. No one returns to health without developing a balanced outlook about the "doing-ness" of their lives. If people work too hard and are under constant stress, they leech vitality and well-being from their energy centers. Knowing when to stop, or when something is enough, is a very important boundary for maintaining health. If these boundaries do not naturally exist because of early abuse issues, it is wise to create them in your mind.

Knowing when something is enough can save vitality and health. The important issue is to know that who you are is enough. If someone does not acknowledge you for what you do, the unconscious inclination is to do more to please them. When we know that we are enough, then we make healthy decisions for our well-being.

Conservation of vitality comes with maturity. Physical regeneration and well-being begin by understanding that what we do and what we have are enough. Taking time out, or a daily rest, giving oneself the space to let down is like applying a preservative. The body heals in sleep and

tranquility. Burning up more adrenaline than one needs to creates serious health hazards.

If you want health it is important to know that the body regenerates with the proper stimulus. The body thrives on medicine compatible with one's higher consciousness. Energetic medicines such as homeopathy, acupuncture, herbalism, and hands-on healing restore natural vitality. Allopathic medicines give the body heroic doses of chemicals that require large quantities of energy to break down and assimilate. Eating food with additives and diminished life force from radiation and spraying only cause the cells to become stagnant with irritants. All this eventually weakens the body's responses.

The Sacral Chakra functions best when there are optimal conditions for joy, relaxation, and pleasure. If the body is used as a beast of burden, it will wear out early and develop painful conditions from the strain. If the body is not given enough stimulation in the form of exercise, it becomes lazy and congested. What is good for the body is good for our energy.

This chakra thrives with a combination of healthy discipline and enough pleasure to ease out stress and tension in the body. It looks for natural solutions that honor the physical being and the spirit of a person. If the Sacral Chakra is looked after properly, the physical body is vital and energetic for well into the senior years. It wears down from a lack of pleasure, harsh and punishing treatment, and physical therapies that do not involve an energetic context for healing.

Below **The crocodile stands for the mythical sea monster that rules the Sacral Chakra. He reminds us that we need food, rest, exercise, and pleasure. When the monster feels deprived of its creature comforts it becomes irritable and unhappy.**

HOW TO ACCESS THE SACRAL CHAKRA

When we honor our physical bodies we affirm our right to pleasure and well-being. We learn to treat ourselves respectfully by giving ourselves peaceful moments that do not brutalize the body by pumping adrenaline into it. Too much of this hormone corrodes the arteries and eats away at the integrity of the cell. It is meant to be used for the fight-or-flight response that is evoked when we find ourselves facing life-threatening situations, not getting to and from our jobs every day. When we develop a wholesome consciousness about our physicality, we help heal and expand the Sacral Chakra. We also help develop reserves of vitality that can be accessed easily when we are stressed or challenged.

Giving ourselves space to express our feelings means that we do not have to deal with the consequences of suppressed emotions. What is unexpressed becomes suppressed in the deep musculature of the body, clogging its elasticity and shortening its capacity to extend fully. Suppressed grief goes into the lumbar region of the back, tightens the chest muscles, and constricts our breathing.

Fear not only eats away at our stomach, making digestion and assimilation difficult, but it is also held in the muscles of the abdomen and mid-back. When we experience those feelings and allow them expression, we help release the body of harmful tension and stress. Instead of using powerful suppressant drugs to stop our anxiety and fear, we learn how to experience our feelings without destroying our vitality and limiting our life force.

Imagine what it would feel like to have high degrees of physical vitality, emotional balance, and mental clarity as well as enough energy left over to be creative and grow internally.

A wholesome lifestyle invites comfort and ease. It also includes the rigor of a healthy exercise program along with good nutrition and downtime to relax and have fun. If we have the attitude that we do not deserve pleasure, we miss the opportunities to bring peace and harmony into our existence.

Experiencing a sense of well-being gives us the opportunity to love life more. With a deeper appreciation for life we naturally become spiritual beings who are grateful to receive the abundance of health, joy, and life itself.

Read out the affirmations in the box below, and allow them to resonate with your spirit. They are designed to bring aliveness and openness to your Sacral Chakra. They encourage you to trust life and know that you do deserve to feel well and experience pleasure.

AFFIRMATIONS FOR THE SACRAL CHAKRA

Repeat these affirmations once every morning and once every evening to bring openness to your Sacral Chakra.

I LOVE MY LIFE
I HONOR MY BODY AND TREAT MYSELF RESPECTFULLY.

I feel the power of healing moving in and through me as I affirm my worth and honor my body.
I trust my feelings and give them ample room for expression.
I lighten my body each time I feel well in myself.
I am a creature of light, open to my highest joy.
I am grateful for the joy of being me.
I receive pleasure and abundance with every breath I take.
Goodness, beauty, and joy resonate with my soul. I am at one with them.
Healing happens each time I rest, relax, and enjoy myself.
My body responds to thoughts of pure love and goodness.
I heal any condition that affects me by knowing my body seeks balance and regeneration.
I stimulate my immunity by knowing God lives in and through me.
I encourage healing each time I affirm my worth and honor my choices for love.
I love who I am exactly as I am.
There is nothing to change about the way I am. As I love and respect myself, healing happens naturally.

As you say them, enjoy the exercise and be playful with the affirmations. You can sing them, even dance them if you like. If you make them a chore, they will carry the energy of drudgery. When we affirm the joy of living, we project that blissful energy into everything we do.

Right **Physical pleasure is vital to balance the needs of the Sacral Chakra.**

Below **The Pyramid is the symbol of the Sacral Chakra. When this energy field is balanced and aligned, our connections to creativity, joy, and abundance are constant.**

MEDITATION FOR
THE SACRAL CHAKRA

When meditating on this center it is important to experience the lower

abdomen and imagine a quality of spaciousness and openness in this area of the

body. Begin by imagining the bones of the pelvis acting as a basin for your vital organs

and a vital link for the spine and leg joints. See the lower spine coming up through the

sacrum and being able to hold the weight of your body. Feel that you are able to carry the

burdens of life and still have enough mobility to move freely and sensuously. Take several deep

breaths deep into the belly, expanding your lower abdomen with every inhalation. As you

release the breath through your mouth, exhale all tension and negativity that has

accumulated in your guts and any sense of disharmony that may be around you. When

you feel ready to begin the meditation, close your eyes and imagine in your mind's eye

a large orange pyramid lodged in your lower abdomen. The apex is pointing up

toward the heart and the base rests on your hip bones.

IMAGINE a large ORANGE pyramid in your lower ABDOMEN

The four walls of this pyramid represent the qualities of

well-being, deservedness, pleasure, and abundance. Expand the form

and intensify the color as you create a healing space for your Sacral Chakra

to rest in. Keep breathing deeply into your belly so that tension is released through

the breath. See each of the four sides of the chakra becoming upright, strong, and

resilient. Know that these boundaries cannot be defiled and will protect your vital energy.

Tell yourself that there will always be enough energy to do the things you enjoy and the

tasks that must be completed.

The far back wall of the chakra represents the quality of well-being. Strengthen it and

expand the walls so they act as a strong brace against the back of your sacrum. Feel

that you have sufficient vitality to move forward in life, doing what you love and

enjoying the process of enfoldment.

The far left-hand side of the pyramid represents the quality of deservedness. This embraces your right to pleasure, abundance, and good health. If you have any doubts about what you deserve, release them and trust that life is meant to be pleasurable and comfortable. Allow this awareness into your consciousness.

Now visualize the front wall of the pyramid. This represents pleasure and your capacity to experience joy. Expand the wall to include your entire pelvis. Hold your physical body within the structure of the pyramid. You know that your body is healing from the past. Whatever negative energy was blocking your capacity for joy is now melting under the warmth and pleasure found in your lower belly. Ease the muscles and breathe deeply, all the way to your pubic bone. Say yes to life and the goodness you know surrounds you.

Now bring your attention to the far right-hand wall of this large orange pyramid. This represents the quality of abundance. Allow the good to flood into your chakra. Expand your sense of abundance to include all the good things that surround you from the sky, sun, moon, and stars. Be thankful for the wind, the rain, and all the beauty of nature. Again, expand the form of the Sacral Chakra and intensify the color.

Now seal the pyramid with a cross of light within a circle of light. This seals and protects the energy of this chakra. Repeat this meditation on a regular basis to develop a healthy and balanced Sacral Chakra.

CRYSTALS

CORNELIAN

This stone, related to the agate family, is the color of the Sacral Chakra. It is meant to promote health and well-being and bring the wearer pleasure and comfort. It can be found on the shores of oceans and lakes, which suggests its close connection to water and the emotions. It acts to stabilize distraught feelings.

ONYX

This stone has a strong magnetic charge and can stimulate healing at a physical level by magnetizing the blood. When it is combined with a Herkamer diamond, which is a very hard quartz crystal, it creates a powerful energetic force that can be used for healing. It is used to help regenerate and recharge the life force.

TIGER'S EYE

This stone is reputed to bring prosperity and abundance. It is a stone that carries good luck and fortune with it and helps in business and negotiations. Wearing it or keeping it near at hand stimulates physical well-being.

QUESTIONNAIRE ON THE SACRAL CHAKRA

The following questions are designed to help you place the qualities of the Sacral Chakra into a healthy context that may better enable you to live a happy and wholesome life. Look at the questions as an opportunity for you to evaluate what you do with your life energy. If you want to implement changes in your life after reviewing these questions, give some consideration to how you can make permanent and sustainable changes that will bring you health and well-being. Remember that recharging your vitality from time to time is essential.

Well-being

- Do you give yourself time off from the grind of daily life? How often in the course of a day do you stop what you are doing and take a break?
- Do you look after your need for nutritious food, enough fluids, vitamin supplements?
- Do you use a form of medicine that is energetically based, rather than chemical inducements?
- Do you honor your body's need for rest when you are tired?
- Do you give yourself a change of scenery from time to time by going out into nature or visiting a healthy environment?
- Do you give your body treatments such as body work, facials, or massage?
- What do you do to alleviate stress in your body?
- How do you cope with the demands on your time and energy?
- Do you know when to say no to those who are toxic and negative?
- Can you protect your vitality from being drained in wasted conversations and highly dramatic events?

Deservedness

- Do you feel you deserve the life you say you want?
- Do you deserve peace, beauty, and tranquility in your life?
- Do you deserve love, kindness, and true friends?

- Do you deserve vacations and holidays where you have an opportunity to recharge your vital force?
- Do you feel you deserve to be recognized as a whole person with individual needs?
- Do you feel that you deserve to enjoy life?
- Do you have doubts or reservations about your deservedness based on the way you have experienced life in your past?
- Do you experience dark moments when you feel you are not "enough" and will always be deficient in the things that matter to you in life? Do you feel you deserve to see yourself as "enough"?
- Do you feel that you can manage external pressures knowing that you deserve time out to live your life the way you choose?
- Do you feel you deserve the happiness you long for?

Pleasure

- How much pleasure do you feel you deserve each day?
- Would you believe that your life can have increased levels of pleasure regularly?
- Do you feel that you can manage to build in pleasure as part of your regular lifestyle?
- To what extent do you try to include joy and pleasure whenever you are planning time for yourself?

- Is pleasure something you trust yourself to enjoy?
- Can you see the joy and pleasure in small things?
- Can you give yourself permission to enjoy what is around you and see the pleasure in looking at the good things in your life?
- Are you able to enjoy the moment?
- Do you complicate your life with too much mental activity?
- Do you overlook the simple and easy way to do things in order to have a big effect on others?

Abundance

- How abundant is your life?
- Do you recognize the degree of prosperity you have been blessed with?
- Are you able to see that abundance in more than the money you have?

THE COLOR OF
THE SACRAL CHAKRA: ORANGE

The color of the Sacral Chakra is orange. This is a hot color, full of vital energy and deeply connected with the life force. It represents sensuality and sexuality, as well as a deep connection to joy and passion. This color stimulates physical energy in the body and can open channels of suppressed vitality from an overactive mind. Wearing this color or painting a shade of it in a room brings warmth, healing, and physical well-being. It is the color that affects appetite. Many restaurants and fast-food chains use it to subconsciously increase appetite.

Above **Pleasure is that connection between the outer world of people and experiences and our inner being. There is a resonance between the subjective and the objective, which delights our being**

- Do you feel that you could manage with less and still feel you had abundance?
- Do you feel you need more money and things to be happy?
- To what degree do you value the things you have now?
- Are you thankful for the goodness that has sustained you?
- Are you able to create a sense of balance between what you have and what you want?
- Can you relax enough to partake in a celebration of life to give thanks for all you see and enjoy?

WORKING THROUGH NEGATIVITY

- Honor the physical body by giving it enough food, water, rest, and exercise.
- Respect the limits of the physical body and do not become trapped in obsessive acts of exertion, pushing the body beyond its natural limits.
- Accept your need for pleasure and create enough good experiences to replenish the spirit as well as the body.
- Acknowledge the powerful force of human sexuality and know what one's values are regarding it.
- Respect the physical world by keeping order, cleanliness, and beauty around your home, office, and places of recreation.
- Reflect upon physical energy you put into earning money and the ways that you make financial decisions.
- Know that you have appetites and needs and give them a place in your experience.
- Treat yourself to the joys of life and know that you deserve what you say you want.

THE SOLAR PLEXUS CHAKRA

MANIPURA

Lustrous jewel

The Solar Plexus Chakra is the center of personal identity. It is the seat of the ego, and develops in our teens and is anchored by our early twenties. The Solar Plexus Chakra rules all aspects of our personality and ego, especially our sense of self-worth, self-esteem, and personal identity. This energy center also influences self-confidence and degrees of personal power, as well as freedom of choice. Ultimately it helps us choose what and who are for our highest good.

The symbol of the Solar Plexus Chakra

Solar Plexus Chakra

QUALITIES AND ATTRIBUTES

Selfhood emerges during our adolescence and is differentiated by the time we reach young adulthood. The Solar Plexus Chakra regulates an inner knowing and gut instincts about things and people. It develops in relationships, work, finances, and areas of self-management and responsibility. As adults, we are required to establish a personal identity that defines who we are. Facing this challenge, our sense of self begins to emerge. This nurtures the Solar Plexus Chakra and makes it expand. As our sense of self grows, a strong and resilient inner core develops.

Self-worth is the primary quality of the Solar Plexus Chakra. Our personal identity, formed in family life, expands in young adulthood so that we can honor ourselves as we interact and negotiate with the world.

Our true self is that part of us that is always whole and intact. It is where truth, beauty, and freedom abide. It is not affected by pain, loss, or trauma. Though life appears difficult at times, we are made whole when we connect to the self. It is an awareness of invaluable worth, esteem, and true power. The self is more radiant than the sun.

Personal power also resides in the Solar Plexus Chakra. It forms from developing an abiding sense of who we are. This power can express itself in any situation and guides us through the maze of resistance and opposition placed in our path to help us grow and mature. It thrives in the realm of resistance to form a strong Warrior archetype able to stand on its own feet and "fight the good fight." Without challenges that develop inner grit, personal power cannot be developed.

Location: Directly below the sternum and over the stomach

Age of resonance: 14–21

Shape: Globe

Glandular connection: Pancreas

Color: Yellow

Musical note: E

Type of music: Marches

Element: Fire

Aspect of intelligence: Instinctual knowing

Sensory experience: Vision

Essential oils: Lemon, grapefruit, juniper

Crystals: Topaz, citrine, amber

Aspects of the solar system: Mars and the Sun

Astrological associations: Aries, Leo

Metals: Iron, gold

Earthly location: United States of America

Mythological animal: Lion

Plant: Carnation

Qualities: Self-worth, self-esteem, confidence, personal power, freedom of choice

Life issues: To develop a strong and resilient ego; to know you are worthy simply because you exist.

Physical activities: Sports, competitive programs, qi gong, hiking, cycling

Spiritual activities: Leadership programs, psychotherapy, amateur dramatics, appreciating solitude

Positive archetype: Warrior

Negative archetype: Servant

Angelic presence: Archangel Uriel, regent of the Sun

ARCHETYPES

POSITIVE: The Warrior

The warrior is an empowered person with a definitive sense of selfhood. Warriors know who they are in themselves and in relation to the world. Their sense of self is neither inflated nor weak. They have the inner strength and resilience to see their dreams materialize into reality and the stamina to meet physical and emotional challenges. They are able to fight the good fight for love, victory, and the glory of God.

NEGATIVE: The Servant

The servant is a person whose sense of personal identity is anchored in the external world, always seeking confirmation from others. Servants work hard for others' acknowledgment. They sabotage themselves by giving their power to others to define who they are and what they need to do. They lose energy trying to please others for the affirmation they are unable to give to themselves.

THE INFLUENCE OF THE SOLAR PLEXUS CHAKRA

The shining light of selfhood reflected in the Solar Plexus Chakra requires that we see the world in a state of duality. This means that there has to be opposition and contradiction to rub against in order for our internal development to take place. From the view of this chakra we will witness life in terms of "us and them" or "others." This duality is how the ego is formed and how it cultivates a sense of itself in the world.

This chakra is the center of our ego, which is our individuality, and the ego always perceives life in terms of duality, frontiers, and boundaries. The Solar Plexus Chakra develops as we formulate our personality and sense of individuality. Without challenges to create a strong internal sense of life, we stagnate and fail to mature. The Solar Plexus Chakra governs the ages from 14 to 21. It culminates at

Above **The Solar Plexus resonates at the time we begin our path into adulthood. Our sense of Self is intact and we begin to know what we wish to pursue in life.**

the time when young people begin their path in life. Some opt for marriage or other love relationships, others take on jobs or start careers. All face entering the world, engaging in relationships, and developing selfhood.

Young adulthood and all new beginnings are governed by this chakra. At this time of life it is appropriate to make mistakes as well as wholesome choices. Each challenge faced helps develop other internal qualities that define selfhood. Confidence and self-worth, as well as personal power, come from meeting the world on your own terms.

These qualities are a natural outflow of the choices we make for ourselves. In young adulthood we learn from trial and error and develop confidence in our ability to stand on our own. Character formation does not come because of our family, our connections, or what we perceive to be our right: it comes out of experience of knowing who we are.

Personal power is the ability to influence others and make changes in any situation. It comes from having done something well with impeccable integrity. When we realize the discipline we put into making things happen in our lives, we choose a path to mastery and the cultivation of personal power. Each time we finish a task, complete a course of action, or stand by someone when the odds are down, we add depth and quality to our personal power. These are all the qualities that define character.

Freedom of choice is the ultimate determination of the Solar Plexus Chakra. The choice to be ourselves, to choose love, respect, and kindness, and to do what we know is right is something that every generation has sacrificed to maintain. We make good decisions for ourselves when we know our worth, have a sense of pride in our efforts, and feel confident about our abilities.

This is how personal power comes about. When all these components are in place, we are able to make wholesome choices

THE SOLAR PLEXUS CHAKRA AND THE PANCREAS

The pancreas is the ductless gland for the Solar Plexus Chakra. On a physical level, the pancreas controls carbohydrate metabolism, including regulating glucose and insulin in the blood. It also influences nutritional absorption. At an esoteric level, the pancreas is concerned with joy. Diabetes, for instance, is felt to be a disease of lack of joy and disempowerment. As we develop a sense of selfhood, our level of joy increases and we experience the power of healing in our emotional and physical well-being.

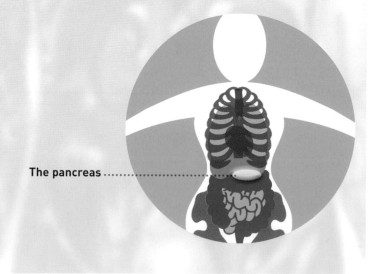

The pancreas ....

that enhance freedom. This is one of the most essential aspects of humanity that we cherish and value.

The Solar Plexus Chakra extends into the realms of the heart. It influences the way we respond to situations through compassion and love. It is especially connected to the heart by how strongly we love and value ourselves. If we are disconnected from our heart we run the risk of becoming manipulative, exploitative, and egotistical. Keeping checks on the ego so that it is connected to the self is both healthy and mature. When the ego gets too strong, a high degree of separation exists between oneself and another, and others are regarded as objects.

Gut instincts are centered in this chakra. How we respond to external influences shows how strong our Warrior archetype is. When we act from a place of strength, able to take control of our lives, and embody heroic qualities that instill confidence and trust in others, we gain power and the ability to influence situations and people. When fear dominates our lives, we lose energy and power and create dependency on others for our well-being.

We have the capacity to heal others as well as ourselves by developing selfhood. This requires formulating a healthy and wholesome personality able to stand on its own. It requires knowing who we really are at the core and making wholesome choices from a place of optimal freedom. Allowing the Solar Plexus Chakra to be all it can be means that we allow ourselves to be the same.

Below **The Sun is one of the ruling elements of the Solar Plexus Chakra.**

HOW TO ACCESS THE SOLAR PLEXUS CHAKRA

64

The Book of Chakras *The Solar Plexus Chakra*

As the center for personal empowerment, the Solar Plexus Chakra can be mastered only when we know our worth and connect to the world through an abiding sense of self. When the ego has a healthy link to the self it negotiates with the world in a balanced and considerate way. It is neither inflated—with an overdeveloped sense of its importance—nor manipulative or exploitative. When the Solar Plexus Chakra is balanced, the ego is strong and effective and confirmed in its worthiness. It is not constantly depending on external stimulation to prove or affirm itself.

When our personal identity is intact we know who we are. We know we are worthy of love, kindness, and respect, and that the world mirrors this sense of worth back to us in relationships, jobs, and what we do in our daily lives. People who don't know who they are act out of a deep need for recognition and attention. Instead of generating peace

AFFIRMATIONS FOR THE SOLAR PLEXUS CHAKRA

Repeat these affirmations once every morning and once every evening to strengthen your Solar Plexus Chakra.

I AM WORTH
MY WEIGHT IN GOLD.

I am worthy of love, kindness, and respect, regardless of what I have done.
I am worthy because I exist.
I am worthy of the life I say I want.
I am worthy of the best.
I am confident in my ability to make my life work.
I am confident in the goodness of life itself to see me through.
I accept the power of my being to produce health, love, and joy in my life.
I know I am a powerful and wholesome force for good.
I choose the power of life.
I choose goodness, light, and love.
I choose health, healing, and happiness.
I choose the best for myself.

and harmony, they often create drama and chaos in their lives and the lives of those around them.

When we know our worth we also know our boundaries. We know we will not tolerate abuse, harm, or destruction. We avoid negativity and stay on a positive, uplifting track to the best of our ability. If fear does surface in our lives, we honor who we are and respect our limits. We look for what is wholesome, good, and healing in life and we appreciate a sense of oneness with all life.

When this chakra is activated and balanced, we make positive choices for our lives. As we grow and develop a strong and resilient ego, we build abundant reserves of energy we can draw on when we are tired, ill, or distressed. We learn to trust our instincts. This chakra has a deep-seated animal intelligence that helps us differentiate between what and who are and are not really good for us. It hones our instinctual nature to choose the light,

Above **This picture is a metaphor for knowing that you are worth your weight in gold. This may help you realize that you are worthy of love, kindness, and respect.**

Left **The Solar Plexus Chakra is the center for personal empowerment. When we accept ourselves and know that we are worthy of love and respect we feel at peace and generate peace around us.**

and to choose what is best not only for ourselves but for those we love.

The nature of the Solar Plexus Chakra is power itself. If power is too strong, this chakra becomes manipulative, exploitative, and dangerous. When it is deflated we see people lose their center and want for the grit to get through challenging situations. In accessing this chakra we learn to deal with issues of power and turn them into loving and positive situations for ourselves. Learning right use of power is essential for this chakra to develop in a healthy way.

This chakra supports psychological growth and development. We all deserve to know how good we truly are, and we all deserve support, kindness, and respect for the simple reason that we exist. Our worth comes with the territory of our humanity because we are innately worthy as human beings to experience our light and enjoy life. Learning this is one of the essential lessons in life. It can bring us great healing from abuse and the freedom to be who we truly are.

Healing this chakra involves strengthening and confirming our sense of self. It takes a deep awareness to know that who we are is not conditional on what we have or what we do. Too many people link their sense of personal identity with being accepted by others. When we know who we are we are less likely to renounce our individuality. We work to cultivate a sense of worth and to make healthy choices that help us to express our truth in our own unique ways.

The affirmations for the Solar Plexus Chakra are designed to regenerate our sense of self and to help us integrate and assimilate a deepened sense of our true worth. If you have issues of doubt, lack of confidence, or low self-esteem, make these affirmations become part of your daily life. You can write or speak them and practice them daily and before you go to bed at night. Heal your feelings of lack so that your sun can shine brightly.

MEDITATION FOR THE SOLAR PLEXUS CHAKRA

In doing the meditation for the Solar Plexus Chakra, it is essential to begin by relaxing and feeling comfortable. Take several large and deep breaths, as though into your stomach, and exhale slowly and completely before resuming another breath. Do this six times before continuing. This area accumulates tension and is often painful and tight in many people. You can rub the abdominal area with your fingers to loosen it as you do this breathing exercise. It helps to be able to sit quietly while you let go of tension. When you feel relaxed you can close your eyes and begin the meditation.

Begin by visualizing a large golden globe that expands out from your belly. Allow this globe to fill your entire abdomen. See the golden light warming you and releasing tension in your stomach, gallbladder, liver, and pancreas. This light reaches into the dark corners of your organs, filling each recess with light. It helps relax even more as tension is released with each breath.

VISUALIZE a large GOLDEN GLOBE that EXPANDS out from your BELLY

Breathe deeply into your body and feel the warmth of your own light take away the stress and pressures you have recently experienced. Know that you are worthy of the life you say you want. Love, prosperity, and goodness are possible for you. Be open to receiving your highest good unconditionally. You need only know that your path to joy is opening as you love and accept who you are. All efforts to prove your worth diminish as you accept your self and honor your right to know and love yourself. Begin to experience confidence in your ability to meet the challenges of your life.

You have the power to see things through to a positive conclusion. Choose to do the best you can. Choose love, light, and healing in all aspects of your life. Allow this light to move in and through you and shine in front of you as you experience your intelligence and love for freedom.

If you feel confused, frightened, or weak, be

assured that you can master your fears and put chaos behind

you. By accepting your spiritual lessons within your surroundings, you will

find the power to change your life.

The Solar Plexus Chakra moves us to excellence just as living tends to cultivate our

character. When our physical, emotional, and mental health is challenged, time should be

taken to firm up our footing. Know that it is our intentions that allow us to achieve what our heart

desires. Be flexible, compassionate, and open to changes. A new approach can be revealed to us

unexpectedly at any time.

When you have expanded the form of the solar plexus, visualize a cross of light within a circle of light.

Whenever you feel too diffuse, spaced out, or frightened, visualize this large golden globe in your

solar plexus and seal it with a cross of light within a circle of light. It will give you protection,

grounding, and a sense of yourself at all times.

CRYSTALS

TOPAZ

This has been the traditional stone of courage and healing. It was found in the breastplate of the high priest Aaron, mentioned in Exodus. It denotes instinctual understanding of life issues and challenges. It brings healing by giving us confidence in ourselves.

AMBER

This is a crystallized resin. It is believed that the sap came from ancient trees that were alive during the Matriarchy, the time in which women held reign over the practicalities of life, were the priests and driving force in the culture. This happened between 15,000 and 750,000 years ago according to some sources. Amber is associated with feminine power and is thought to be a stone for women finding their internal empowerment.

CITRINE

This stone combines the yellow found in the Solar Plexus and the green in the Heart Chakra. It is the color of spring shoots and suggests transition, new beginnings and an awakening of the heart. It is used to stabilize love of oneself by honoring our personal choices for growth and spirituality.

QUESTIONNAIRE ON THE SOLAR PLEXUS CHAKRA

The questions concerning the Solar Plexus Chakra are divided into the qualities that govern this center. Take your time in answering them and work to develop these qualities if they are weak or underdeveloped in you. They will help generate a strong sense of selfhood that will give you strength and stamina in challenging situations.

This chakra looks toward heroic efforts to help you become the best you can be. Often life challenges can undermine our physical, emotional, and mental health and time may be required to put us back on a strong footing before we can resume our life. Know that if you are intent you will achieve whatever you set your heart on. Be flexible, compassionate, and open to changes that may reveal a better way of doing things. Life is a wonderful opportunity to cultivate your character. Allow your sense of self to expand with each situation that demands presence, steadiness, and character.

Self-worth

- How strongly do you value yourself?
- Do you know the ultimate worth of selfhood?
- Do you honor your sense of who you are in situations with family and friends?
- Do you hide your innate sense of worth from others because you think you will be different?
- Do you see worth in others when they don't see their own light shining?
- Can you connect within yourself to this place of light, intelligence, and love?
- Are you willing to take the time and do the inner work to cultivate a strong anchor to your selfhood?

Self-esteem

- What things are you the most proud of having done in your life?
- Do you feel that you can value past achievements?
- Do you respect yourself for having done a good job at certain things in life?
- What do you consider to be the finest thing you have done in your life?

Above **The first three chakras are concerned with family, tribe, clan, and country. They help us individuate and find our sense of personal identity.**

- What do you consider to be the kindest thing you have ever done?
- Are you willing to acknowledge yourself for being able to see something through to its conclusion, especially if it was difficult and challenging?

- What are the consequences of your having put yourself on the line to accomplish a task?
- Do you value your ability to do good?

Confidence

- Are you confident in your ability to do something well?
- Are you pleased by the way you can choose to do a project and complete it?
- Are you confident in your ability to make necessary changes in your life?
- Are you confident that you see a good opportunity when it presents itself to you?
- Are you confident in your ability to communicate your needs to those around you and be understood?
- Are you confident in your ability to make good choices for yourself in relationships?
- Are you confident that you will succeed in your tasks and with things that are important to you?

Personal power

- What is your relationship to your own power?

Below **When we take responsibility for our feelings of anger or joy, we know that we are entitled to them and we reclaim both confidence and power.**

- Are you willing to exert your personal power if you feel wronged or abused?
- Are you willing to express yourself in a powerful way that lets others know not to mess with you?
- Are you able to use your personal power to make something happen that would make life better for others?
- Are you clear about your need to balance your personal power with humility and compassion?
- Do you abuse your personal power by being irritated and difficult with those not in a position to challenge you?
- Do you cultivate your personal power and learn to temper it when appropriate?
- Do you honor your power by using it only when necessary?

Freedom of choice
- Do you know that you are always free to choose in every situation?
- Do you exercise your freedom to choose to be yourself at all times?
- Do you honor this gift and defend it when asked to make a decision?
- Do you realize that freedom of choice is essential to your human development?
- Do you prize this gift above all others given you by God and defended by your country?
- Do you experience freedom when you make a choice for the good in your life?

THE COLOR OF THE
SOLAR PLEXUS CHAKRA: YELLOW

Yellow contains more light than any color in the visible spectrum. It is associated with the sun and the metal gold. It is a diffuse color, which creates confusion with overexposure. Because there is so much light in yellow one can become disoriented as well as cheered. Yellow is a warm color that gives off heat, though less intensely than orange or red. It lifts the spirit and gives hope, as well as a sense of ease and lightness.

Yellow is associated with fire energy, which can break down other elements. We need this color and the element of fire to break down nutrients in the body so that they can be absorbed. We need this color to create a proper mental framework so that we can digest new ideas.

WORKING THROUGH NEGATIVITY

- **Develop a sense of your own person. Know that who you are is always the same, even in a variety of circumstances.**
- **Create your own sense of personality that lets others know who you are.**
- **Following the crowd may be safe but it will always be limiting and stultifying.**
- **Spend time alone with yourself. Learn to cultivate your own friendship.**
- **Ask yourself if you are worthy of the life you say you want.**
- **Find out where your talents and gifts lie.**
- **Don't be afraid to try new things. Experience of self develops from placing yourself in challenging situations.**
- **Travel and exploration help define you in the face of adversity and challenge.**
- **Learn to recognize character and integrity in yourself and others.**

THE HEART CHAKRA
ANAHATA
Unstruck

The Heart Chakra governs the physical heart and lungs. It is essential to our physical supply of energy and vitality as well as the love that nourishes our spiritual existence. Centering ourselves in love gives our life purpose and meaning. It anchors us in Selfhood, which is love itself. What this means, on a real level, is that our very nature is loving, kind, and respectful. Growth and healing open a panorama, where we give love freely and unconditionally and receive it in the same way.

The symbol of the Heart Chakra

Heart Chakra

QUALITIES AND ATTRIBUTES

The Heart Chakra is partially open in early childhood and closes down as we mature and become products of our culture. If there was a lack of love in the beginning of life it can be difficult to allow the heart to open. At some point in early adulthood, around age 28, the Heart Chakra seeks to expand, longing for love. It searches for ways in which it can open. Certain experiences trigger this blossoming: relationships forged, children born, choices made that let us love ourselves better. At this age the heart is ready to engage in real and mature love, for the self and others. Not to allow this natural evolution obstructs normal development.

The pull of sex, power, and money pales in comparison with the joys of the heart. Love is something that stays in our hearts forever. Being willing to experience lasting love, rather than indulge in temporary attractions, is the significance of the Heart Chakra.

The qualities of the Heart Chakra are peace, love, unity, brotherhood and sisterhood, and joy. All these aspects of the heart speak of love of life and a penetrating awareness of the sacredness of all things. The heart thrives on joy and delight; it flourishes on openness, sharing, touch, and connection. It contracts with pain, loss, and trauma. Feeding the heart with positive energy is choosing to see the love in people, and the joy in all things.

The message of the Heart Chakra is to accept the oneness of all life. Through loving we radiate the joy of being. An open Heart Chakra is experienced by others as warm, inviting, and tender. An old Irish saying goes, "Find people who warm you." This refers to seeking a true heart connection with others.

Location: Middle of the chest
Age of resonance: 28–35
Shape: Crescent moon
Glandular connection: Thymus gland
Color: Green for the heart protector,
        pink or gold for the heart itself
Musical note: F
Type of music: Choral
Element: Air
Aspect of intelligence: Remembering
        the good, loving, and caring
Sensory experience: Touch
Essential oils: Rose, carnation,
        lily of the valley
Crystals: Rose quartz, diamond, peridot
Aspects of the solar system: Venus
        and the Sun
Astrological associations: Libra and
        Taurus
Metals: Copper and gold
Earthly location: Spain
Mythological animal: Deer
Plants: Foxglove, rose, carnation, lily
Qualities: Unity, brotherhood/sisterhood,
        love, peace, purity, and innocence
Life issues: To let love be the center of your life
Physical activities: Yoga, massage, healing
        touch, walking, dancing
Spiritual activities: Learning to love yourself
        first, then others, prayer, healing, singing,
        joyful endeavor
Positive archetype: Lover
Negative archetype: Actor/actress
Angelic presence: Archangel Raphael

POSITIVE: The Lover

This is a person whose ground of being is centered in the heart. They love unconditionally, and heal the tight, hard places in those they touch because they bring warmth and acceptance. They generate goodness and are genuinely embracing and kind. Their love is inclusive, uniting those on the outside. They share love with everyone. They know that to love is to live. Knowing this archetype changes your life for the good.

NEGATIVE: The Actor/Actress

This is a person whose love is conditional. They have expectations about the how and whom they can love. If someone falls outside of the realm of their conditions they withhold their love. They love in the limited way they have been loved, with judgment, and criticism for what doesn't fit into their framework. They love through imitation rather than true feeling. Their relationships often dry up because they have not developed a capacity to hold love in their hearts.

THE INFLUENCE OF THE HEART CHAKRA

Deep healing comes through the Heart Chakra. This is where, according to mystics, God lives within each of us. Our heart song resonates with the pulse of our being. As we evolve we long for a heart connection in all things. It gives us a sense of unity and belonging; it helps us share the best of ourselves with others.

The heart suffers whenever there is a sense of separation or isolation. For the heart to heal we employ forgiveness, prayer, meditation, and positive intent to release old hurts that weigh us down and perpetuate the illusion of our singularity.

Once we transcend the lower chakras and come into the realm of the heart, there is only oneness. Power, sex, and money no longer hold a thrill or sustain our feelings. Joy comes when we are connected to love, unity, and peace. Removing impediments to the experience of love takes love itself,

Left **Nourish the heart by spending time in nature. She is the supreme healer, giving us the space to breathe clean air, and find tranquility and beauty.**

Below **Joy comes when we are connected to another. Love feeds us, heals us, and lets us know that its fulfillment is our highest purpose on this earth plane.**

especially for oneself. This love may take the form of seeking help from a teacher, therapist, or friend. It implies it is time to fill the heart with love and release any sense of inferiority, unworthiness, and lack.

Getting to the core of the heart means becoming aware that who we are and what we do are love itself. There is no divisibility here. In the realm of heart we are connected to the divine heart.

A strong heart is able to forgive the wounds of the past, find joy in the moment, and step into the world to make it a better place. We fight the good fight for "love, victory and the glory of God," as Paulo Coelho says in his books. Our path toward love keeps us light, positive, and open to our highest good. The great Satguru, Sri H. W. L. Poonja, says our spiritual challenge is to love the self and have the heart of a lion through the thick and thin of life. As we gracefully surrender to life we allow it to move us and with an open heart we accept ourselves and others in divine grace.

The heart's unique intelligence is to remember love. It never forgets acts of kindness, friendship, or love. Being loved, accepted, and nourished is how we manage

to go forward in life. If we don't receive this from an external source our growth process is to learn to give it to ourselves. When the mind chooses to dwell on the negative, the destructive, and the abusive, the heart is leeched of what it needs to survive. It only wants to remember the good and the joyful and feel love in the present moment.

The mind, by its very nature, is divisive and creates the illusion of duality. The heart unifies, and brings together the threads of love, whether from those closest to us or the kindness of strangers. The heart's work is to be receptive and allow love to be.

The heart is nourished by peace and is kept happy and stable. It is important to nourish the heart by spending time in silence, in nature, and with positive people. It helps to read uplifting books and to cultivate laughter and play in one's life. Doing what makes your heart sing keeps the heart strong and alive. An open heart receives as much as it gives.

We revive a wounded heart by our ability to see the good, and forgive the past. This helps us regain energy that has gone into suppressed feelings. Each step toward reconciliation with our self helps release vitality that we can use for creative living. Reconciliation means forgiving the past and living in the present.

The Heart Chakra is made up of two distinct components. The heart protector corresponds to the pericardium (a double-walled sac that surrounds the heart) and acts to protect the heart from external assault. It keeps unwanted criticism, negative thoughts, and impure intentions away from the purity and innocence of the heart.

We forge a strong heart protector by developing an uncompromising love of Self which is reflected in healthy boundaries, and knowing who and what are for our highest good. Our hearts are nourished by love of nature, animals, children, and the elderly. Loving our lives, loving others, and sharing this light heals us and heals the world.

The second component to the Heart Chakra is the heart itself. It is pure, innocent,

THE HEART CHAKRA AND THE THYMUS GLAND

This gland is found in the upper chest. At birth and in early childhood it is almost the size of a small child's fist. It serves as an important component in preserving immunity. As we age, it shrinks. Today it is of interest to science as we see more autoimmune-deficiency diseases, and extracts are now being used to boost the immune system. The thymus gland has a relationship to our emotional well-being. When we are happy and expressing love in our lives, it functions well, secreting hormones that tone the heart and keep the lungs active.

When we are not happy the thymus becomes underactive. It fails to thrive. Energy from the Heart Chakra nourishes this gland. When the heart is open the gland functions well. When the heart is closed the gland shuts down. Living in a state of joy, finding people, things, and activities that make your heart sing keeps the thymus healthy.

Thymus extract or homeopathic preparations can be used whenever there has been loss, rejection, or painful emotional trauma. It keeps the immune system balanced and prevents physical breakdown, which often occurs after an emotional heartache.

Thymus gland

and unblemished. It is the eternal abode of the Holy Spirit in each individual. Knowing the depth, purity, and beauty each individual has been graced with in life can only make us mindful of the jewel that rests in each person's heart. Awakening the connection to that place of love and purity takes love and trust in God, however one chooses to define the Infinite Intelligence that guides our spirit. Seeking that outside of ourselves will only lead us back to where we have started our search, within our own heart.

Right **The heart remembers acts of kindness. We may not be consciously aware of the love that was shown to us when we were younger but love experienced stays in our soul forever.**

Mending the heart so that it is able to love again is the basis of all healing. We all need love as the essential core of our lives, and, if painful wounds have closed the heart off from receiving, it is essential to revive it. The realization that we are love helps ease the pain of rejection or loss. Developing compassion for those who are not able to love us in the way we desire is the awareness of an awakened heart.

Spiritual enlightenment is the awareness that we are love. What we seek in the external world is a mere reflection of our true nature. When we know we are love, then love finds its way into our lives. When we release dark feelings that block the Heart Chakra, we open the channel for love to find us.

AFFIRMATION FOR THE HEART CHAKRA

Repeat this affirmation once every morning and once every evening when you wish to access your Heart Chakra.

ALL LOVE
RESIDES WITHIN MY HEART.

I am quiet and listen to my heart's song.
I choose to be united with all beings, visible and invisible, in the realm of love and light.
I anchor my heart in truth, love, and God's grace.
Love opens and heals me.
I choose the peace that surpasses all understanding.
I am love, I am peace, I am light.
I follow my heart's desire for truth and goodness and love.
My core is pure and innocent. Nothing can touch the soul of my heart except love itself.
God's love fills me and opens my heart to all goodness.
Joy is my reason for living.
I look for the joy in myself and see it in all things.
I delight in sharing my joy.
I let my heart shine and give from the depths of my being to those who accept love.

Above **Mother's love is the first unconditional loving experience we have in life. It is the strongest bond we experience until we find someone in our adult life who offers us companionship, trust, and sharing.**

Left **When our heart is broken our vital energy goes back into the Solar Plexus to strengthen our sense of selfhood and to allow the heart to regain its sense of trust, hope, and strength for when we are able to love again.**

One of the primary principles of healing is first to love ourselves. We do more to mend our wounded heart by accepting our own love and the recognition of wholeness. From that point we are free to choose to love others, and cultivate good relationships that nourish and feed us. When we know there is nothing wrong with us and that love connections fail because others are unable to love, we toughen up and build a stronger heart protector. We also begin to look for people who live according to their hearts and want love in their lives.

We are all entitled to the love we say we want. If we feel a need to limit love by placing conditions on it and controlling the way in which it comes to us we will never know the thrill of experiencing a deep love. It comes from nature, plants, animals, and the world around us. In fact, it is everywhere; we only need to open our hearts to feel it. By its very nature, love is unlimited, unconditional, and free.

The power of the heart to heal itself speaks of the strength of love. When we love ourselves, our creator, and life, things have a miraculous way of unfolding for the good. Faith in the power of love has seen people through the worst of times, and they have been strengthened and made whole by it through difficult and challenging times.

A large part of our healing is accepting that we are lovable and worthy of God's love. To know we are cherished is to acknowledge that love is all around us; it is the very fiber of life. When we surrender to love we allow the ultimate reality to carry us through.

Left **Good relationships nourish and feed us. They teach us how valuable love is in our lives and ask that we honor those who bring us joy, honesty, and trust in a consistent way over time. Good relationships are the real treasures of life.**

MEDITATION FOR
THE HEART CHAKRA

Meditating on the Heart Chakra is done in two parts. First we experience the nature of the heart protector, which acts as a shield from negativity. The qualities of the heart protector are love, joy, unity, brotherhood and sisterhood, and peace. They can act as an invincible shield against the challenges we face throughout life. Follow the instructions in the meditation for developing a strong and resilient heart protector. If you are easily hurt and sensitive to external influences, practicing this meditation on a regular basis will fortify your heart protector. A strong heart protector protects the purity and innocence of your heart.

The second part of this meditation focuses on the heart itself. The heart is always pure and innocent. Taking time to feel the depth of your heart will open your connection to the spiritual realm. Allow the heart to be easy and to have as much rest and joy as you can give yourself. Sit comfortably with your back straight. Take several deep breaths and begin to relax.

visualize a GREEN crescent MOON across your upper CHEST

Let your jaw be free and loose, and let your tongue relax in your mouth. Let your eyes relax and move deeper into your skull. If you feel any tension, breathe into that area of your body and tell it to relax. When you are at ease, begin to visualize a green crescent moon that goes across your upper chest from shoulder blade to shoulder blade. Expand the form and intensify the color. This is the heart protector, which provides a safe haven for the pure and gentle spirit of the heart. You can inflate this protector by strengthening your sense of love, peace, unity, and brotherhood, and feeling your joy.

Visualize a scene in nature where you are surrounded by beauty. Keep your attention here until you feel ready to move on. Enjoy the peace and healing that nature gives us with her beauty. As you hold this vision feel safe and protected from harm. Feel your heart, which you can visualize as either pink or gold, and let it expand as its precious energy fills your entire being with grace.

You may experience a lightness of being and

a sense of resiliency and a knowing that you have enough love

in you to heal the entire world.

The heart is the cave where God dwells within you. You may rest quietly in knowing that this connection is always with you. Know that you are loved, guided, and protected at all times. You can gently leave your ego at the door of this cave and let your consciousness enter within its confines. As you step inside, see the diamond of your self brilliantly lighting up the inside of your heart. This diamond represents the light of your self, that part of you that is eternal and is the heart of God within you. It is beyond time, beyond form, and beyond circumstance. It simply is. As you honor that, know that you are always connected to this place within. You can access it at any time. Here is all love, all light, and all goodness. It is you. As you come out of your meditation be sure to seal the Heart Chakra with a cross of light within

a circle of light. This seals in the energy of the heart space and allows it to bring you healing.

Take your time coming back into your waking reality. Look at yourself in the mirror and

acknowledge that you are the love you feel. Take your gentleness out into the world

and let it be reflected back at you. You have the power to bless all that you

see and wish it well.

CRYSTALS

ROSE QUARTZ

This is a semiprecious stone that stands for love. It is found to resonate with the energy of the Heart Chakra. Its color soothes tension in the heart and brings the vibration of love to all who wear it or keep it near them. Used in a room, it keeps the energy loving and kind.

DIAMOND

This most precious of all gemstones stands for fidelity, loyalty, and divine love. It represents the truth of God's eternal love and is used in wedding rings to signify eternal, undying love, and commitment.

PERIDOT

This semiprecious stone contains the energy of young spring shoots. It mixes the sense of selfhood found in yellow with the balance, tranquility, and unity of green. It brings healing to a fragmented personal identity and stimulates confidence and love of self.

QUESTIONNAIRE ON THE HEART CHAKRA

These questions are designed to let you evaluate your Heart Chakra. See them as a guide to further development. They are only meant to assist you to see the love in your life.

Try not to judge experiences that you have felt were less than wholesome. Love, on a grand scale, may be working in your life by protecting you from people and situations that could have been harmful to you. Putting our past in a proper perspective helps us to open our hearts to the present. Blessing those who have hurt us is an act of forgiveness. It frees us from placing our energy in something that is behind us and brings it into current time.

It is in the now that all love exists. Be gentle with yourself as you look at these questions. Allow love to flow as a constant factor in your relationships with people. Even if your love is not actively received it is not lost. Love and caring intentions are always influencing others, so bless the past and set it free.

HEART PROTECTOR

Love

- ○ Do you feel love for yourself?
- ○ Do you feel love for others in your life?
- ○ Do you feel love for the beauty of nature and animal life around you?
- ○ Do you feel love for life in general?
- ○ What makes your heart sing?
- ○ What gives you a sense of joy?
- ○ Do you love sharing the things that you deeply care about?
- ○ Can you offer up your love to the world around you?
- ○ Can you remember the people in your life you deeply loved?
- ○ Can you forgive those who hurt you in the past?

Peace

- ○ How much peace do you create in your life?
- ○ Do you have peace of mind? Place?
- ○ Do you cultivate peace?
- ○ Do you need to fill your life with experiences and people who are not peaceful?
- ○ What gives you a sense of peace? Is it music? Nature? Quiet? Painting?
- ○ How important is peace in your

Above **We learn love, in its purest sense, from the archetypes of history and religion. The Madonna and Child are the symbol of divine love made flesh. They imply purity of heart and innocence.**

personal life? In your professional life?
- ◉ What can you do to ensure that you will have the peace you need?
- ◉ Do you long for peace and feel it is elusive?
- ◉ Do you need to make changes in your life that will allow more peace in?

- ○ Do you honor the part of you where peace exists within you?

Brotherhood/sisterhood

- ○ Do you believe that we are all connected and one at the core?
- ○ Do you see the people around you as your equals in life?
- ○ Do you recognize that everyone is connected to you?
- ○ Do you see through the social and cultural constraints that limit your accessibility to others?
- ○ Do you feel in your heart that all people are brothers/sisters?
  - ○ Knowing this, can you allow this consciousness to enter into the way you behave with others?
  - ○ Can you sense when something honors this connection or exploits it?
  - ○ Can you share your sense of brotherhood/sisterhood openly, or do you feel you need to withhold your communal spirit because people will take advantage of you?

- How could you do more to foster the sense of brotherhood/sisterhood that you do have?
- Knowing we are all connected allows you to appeal to this part of another when you experience separation from them. Do you know how to access this connection?

Unity

- How do you experience oneness? Is it a mental concept or do you feel this is true?
- How would you honor this sense of unity in your personal life?
- How would you foster unity in your work life?
- How would you teach unity to young children?
- Can you feel a sense of unity with the natural world? With animals? With strangers?
- How do you know we are united? At what level do you think this is so?
- Do you feel that the universe is one with all life?
- If you believe in unity then are you aware of the delusion of separation?
- Can you see the falsehood behind any sense of separation?

Joy

- Where do you find joy in your life?
- What would you do to cultivate more joy?
- Can you define joy and what it feels like?
- Can you allow more joy to be part of your life?
- Do you find joy with people? In nature? In the animal kingdom?

Left **Nelson Mandela is a great symbol for the Heart Chakra. He offers the world peace, joy, and gratitude, all qualities we can try to cultivate in our personal lives for healthier relationships and more wholesome experiences.**

WORKING THROUGH NEGATIVITY

- Finding the love for oneself, in spite of whatever may have happened in the past, brings healing and releases the past.
- Being able to forgive the past, including those who were hurtful, abusive, or destructive, helps keep the heart open.
- Accept the present as the point of power where love can heal our wounds and restore our sense of wholeness.
- Remember that we are all children in the eyes of God. We are one people and one planet, and our spiritual purpose is to allow ourselves to be loved.
- Learning to accept ourselves as we are, without pride or pretense, keeps the heart open and allows the good to come to us.
- Make a list of what makes your heart sing. Commit yourself to the process of reanimating joy by doing what you love, with people you love.
- Seeing the good in even the worst of situations and the most difficult of people helps keep the heart energy alive.

THE COLORS OF THE HEART CHAKRA: GREEN AND PINK

Green is the most neutral color in the visible spectrum. It contains the warmth of yellow and the coolness of blue. It is the color that brings balance, soothing the nerves and acting as a tonic when we are weary, fatigued, or depressed. Nature gives us her healing power through this color more than any other. It was known in ancient times that this color could heal and was especially soothing to the eyes. Monks making copied illuminations used to hold green beryl up to their eyes to relieve eye strain. Green is seen directly on the eyeball, whereas yellow is seen outside the eye and blue is seen in the interior of the eye. It engenders peace and tranquility and is used for clothing and decoration for that purpose

Pink is an essential color for the Heart Chakra. It is the color of mother love and is found in the aura of all babies and young children. Pink is soft, sweet, and soothing. It is good for the heart to see this joyful color. Pink lifts the emotions, purifies the spirit, and generates a tender quality, suggesting approachability. It is used in men's fashion and home decoration more, which implies we are evolving to a space of the heart.

THE THROAT CHAKRA
VISHUDDHA
Purification

The Throat Chakra is the first energetic center that differentiates man from all other life forms. In the ancient Kabbalah, man is referred to as "The Speaker." This single human attribute gives us the power to express ourselves on every level of experience. To honor this gift fully, we are asked to consciously commit to expressing our truth and sing the song of individuality clearly and with integrity. To do so truly serves our spirits.

The symbol of the Throat Chakra

Throat Chakra

QUALITIES AND ATTRIBUTES

The Throat Chakra is the gateway to higher spiritual realms and is called "the mouth of God" in esoteric teachings. This refers to a point on the back of the neck, near the *medulla oblongata* (the lowest part of the brain in vertebrates), where higher spiritual energy is channeled into the body. This occurs when the mind is free and the spirit open. It is where angels whisper in our ears and spiritual inspiration gives our lives meaning and cohesion.

The Throat Chakra is a vessel for subtle energy and its integrity can be harmed through injury and emotional and physical abuse. The Throat Chakra shuts down from grief and unexpressed feelings such as anger and fear. It is compromised when we are dishonest, maligning, or gossip about others. The chakra is damaged by all forms of substance abuse that pass through the throat. Alcohol, smoking, both recreational and allopathic drugs, and over-eating all pass through the narrow opening of the throat and profoundly disrupt the energy flowing from the lower chakras to the Brow and Crown Chakras.

Substance abuse diminishes the will and prevents us from fully harnessing our vitality. It mutes our feelings and confuses and disorients our mind. It cuts us off from expressing our highest truths when they are most needed.

We default on our integrity when we fail to honor our individuality. To maintain a strong and viable sense of Selfhood it is essential to express our truth as best we can, even at the risk of being different or standing apart from others. True adulthood is learning to mean what we say.

Location: The internal and external throat

Age of resonance: 35–42

Shape: An inverted pyramid, suspended around the jaw and pointing down toward the heart

Glandular connection: Thyroid and parathyroid glands

Color: Turquoise

Musical note: G

Type of music: Opera

Element: The ethers, in which all things are contained

Aspect of intelligence: Will and expression

Sensory experience: Hearing

Essential oils: Blue chamomile, gardenia, ylang ylang

Crystals: Turquoise, blue agate, aquamarine

Aspects of the planetary system: Mercury

Astrological associations: Gemini, Virgo

Metal: Mercury

Earthly location: Italy

Mythological animal: Sparrow hawk

Plant: Gardenia

Qualities: Will, communication, creativity, truthfulness, integrity

Life issues: To harness your will, to express your highest truth, to live creatively

Physical activities: Alexander technique, yoga, osteopathic alignment of the spine, cranio-sacral therapy, expressive theater and dance, qi gong, tai chi

Spiritual activities: Chanting, silent retreats, fasting, yoga, prayer, meditation, singing, keeping a journal, public speaking, bearing witness

Positive archetype: Communicator

Negative archetype: Silent child

Angelic presence: Archangel Gabriel, who brings the word of God

ARCHETYPES

POSITIVE: THE COMMUNICATOR

This is a person who lives from personal integrity. Communicators tell the truth to the best of their ability. They are skilled in putting words to their feelings and they are able to stand up for what they believe. They say no when they need to and their word can be trusted.

NEGATIVE: THE SILENT CHILD

This is a person who has suppressed expressiveness because of fear or shame. These people hide their feelings and are not connected to their higher truth. They say yes when they mean no.

The Throat Chakra directly affects the quality of our communication. It is linked to our personal integrity and sense of honor. When we mean what we say and stand by our word we influence the way in which people perceive us. They pay attention to what we say and recognize who we are. As we deepen our commitment to expressing the truth, the Throat Chakra expands and becomes an invincible ally of the spirit, channeling energy for our physical vitality and spiritual development. We become stronger in ourselves and more resilient in our thinking when we express the truth. This provides us with sufficient energy to accomplish our purpose in life.

The reason we have more energy is that a strong Throat Chakra acts as a container for vital energy, keeping it intact so that energy doesn't drain away or become stagnant. When we live from our integrity and communicate honestly an energetic seal forms around the Throat Chakra and energy flows throughout the physical, mental, and emotional centers.

The energetic leaks of a dysfunctional Throat Chakra are experienced as fatigue, weakness, or dissipation. On a physical level this manifests as an underfunctioning thyroid gland. Medication may be prescribed but this doesn't change or alter the leak: it actually makes it larger. Conventional medicine only stimulates the thyroid and causes it to overproduce hormones. Energetically, it has been found that it is essential to express a higher truth and connect to one's spirit for energy to be freely flowing in the system and for the ductless glands to secrete proper levels of hormones.

How we live and express our being directly influences the amount of energy we have for our lives. The Throat Chakra is also connected to willpower. Some people may find that they have to harness their will in order to accomplish simple daily tasks. The will is meant to be used for those spiritual trials that take us to higher levels, but that may be a challenge to our body. You can conserve the will for spiritual development if you are not using it for daily activity. To resonate joy and creativity in your job, relationships, or other aspects of your life, you must be spiritually truthful. You may be suppressing feelings that could

Below left **George Washington is a national archetype for honesty and integrity, both substantial qualities that depict a strong and resilient Throat Chakra. Honesty helps us to remain true to our inner self and take a stand for what we know to be right.**

Below **The delicate fabric of the Throat Chakra is damaged by lying, malicious gossip, and substance abuse, all of which pass through the mouth and throat. These activities weaken the energetic quality of the chakra.**

indicate a need for change. Tuning into your higher truth helps conserve willpower for the challenges that really matter.

Harnessing the will fortifies the Throat Chakra. It helps keep you on the path of honest expression and helps develop character. In terms of a high feel-good factor, truth, energy, and emotions are all interconnected to the life of the body. Saying no to what and who may be harmful is essential to cultivating a strong will.

This chakra is directly linked to the higher self—that exalted aspect of being that offers guidance and protection. One's personal task is to tune in and listen to this guidance. If you are too busy listening to external chatter, or idly talking about other people, the guidance from the higher self gets lost in the cacophony. Unfortunately, the internal auditory system is polluted with negativity from noise, lies, and hyper-exaggeration.

The Throat Chakra also governs the ears. We strengthen this chakra when we listen carefully to our inner voice. Our ability to listen silently opens the Throat Chakra and fortifies the link to the self. It has long been known that sound has the power to heal and can even strengthen the immune system. Hearing positive things about ourselves has a healing effect. Saying affirmations out loud, for instance, has a direct effect on the endorphin levels in our blood.

Hearing we are beautiful and everyone loves us lets our spirits shine. It tells us we are good and lovely. When we hear negativity about ourselves we contract and separate from our core. If we are attached to external acknowledgment from others, we may believe what is said rather than know our own worth.

The power of the Throat Chakra is only as strong as our internal connection to the truth. If we are willing to be quiet and listen to our inner voice it can act as a guiding force in our lives. We can expand the power of our internal guidance when we take the lid off our feelings and simply recognize them for what they are. This means allowing emotions to be experienced, though not necessarily acted out. Emotional suppression

THE THROAT CHAKRA AND THE THYROID GLAND

The function of the thyroid gland is to regulate the basal metabolism, which has a direct effect on regulating the body's growth. It helps in developing teeth, enhancing muscular tone, and aids in mental development. It promotes the functional development of the sexual organs and the adrenal glands.

Thyroid gland ································

stops energy from flowing and it also keeps us from knowing our inner truth.

When the chakra is open and flowing, our inner beauty and external radiance flow freely. It takes someone who knows who they are and what they value to develop a strong Throat Chakra. It demands a willingness to overcome fear of speaking out and a desire to be emotionally mature and psychologically responsible.

Developing a wholesome relationship to the truth is the beginning of healing the Throat Chakra. Nearly all dysfunctional emotional experiences are suppressed in the throat. This happens when we fail to say what we feel, no matter how hurt or angry we are. We begin our empowerment when we tell the truth.

People can be completely changed by the experience of connecting to the truth. Energy, vitality, beauty, and a zest for life suddenly spring into their body and face. They know that speaking the truth connects them to that place within where they are truth itself.

Below **Our ability to communicate clearly determines the quality of our experiences. It also reflects the degree of intention we have to be understood and supported in life. These are essential qualities of the Throat Chakra.**

HOW TO ACCESS THE THROAT CHAKRA

There are many ways in which to open up the throat. If feelings and true expression have been suppressed, one can benefit from therapy to help reanimate the feeling function. Singing or voice lessons are another way of strengthening the throat. Each time the throat is exercised, emotions rise to consciousness. Making a clear intention to express the truth paves the way for healing to happen. Remember that a lifetime of lies, half-truths, and unexpressed emotions damages the Throat Chakra.

Most people are disconnected from their inner reality. They don't know what they are experiencing within themselves. It takes a conscious effort to be comfortable with feelings. If you feel angry, sad, anxious, or joyful, it serves your development to

Above **Listening to the sound of your own voice can help you express yourself. Tape yourself reading your affirmations out loud and then play them back to yourself while you sleep.**

acknowledge these emotional states. Each time you can tell the truth about your feelings, you have the opportunity to look at a deeper truth about the nature of reality.

It always helps us to realize what we feel because it leads us to a better understanding of who we are. Being on the receiving end of insults or attacks, even those subtle put-downs made in jest, diminishes the spirit and weakens self-esteem. The spirit is not enlivened or supported by insult or humiliation. It is important to convey to those close to us that we are not willing to receive the brunt of their displeasure. This is a big step to communicating the truth.

All this implies that we love who we are sufficiently to know our spirit is worth protecting. Insults and snide remarks are always said by people who have an inflated idea of who they are and a diminished sense of others. They seldom realize their statements have a sting. Each time we let a remark pass without acknowledging our feelings we numb ourselves and close off our throat.

When we honor our personal truth and say how we feel, we grow internally. We detach from the need to please others and learn to nurture the spirit. This is transformation that is congruent with maturity and psychological development. Affirming our worth and honoring the choices we have personally made for happiness, health, and our welfare lets others know we are worthy of consideration. Speaking up, no matter how difficult it may seem, gives us confidence in who we are and conserves our vitality and integrity. Letting others get away with negative acts does not serve their integrity, either.

You can begin to heal the Throat Chakra by using affirmations. Saying affirmations out loud is an excellent way to begin this process. It works best to stand in front of a

AFFIRMATIONS FOR THE THROAT CHAKRA

Repeat this affirmation once every morning and once every evening to strengthen and heal the Throat Chakra.

I LIVE IN MY TRUTH,
I COMMUNICATE MY TRUTH, I AM THE TRUTH.

Communicating is vital to my well-being.
I love to share my experiences and tell my truth.
I listen to the truth of others; I share my truth honestly.
My willpower is aligned with my spiritual purpose in life.
I develop will each time I meet a life challenge.
I express my truth as creatively as possible.
I communicate with those who open their hearts to me.
I learn to listen to myself and trust my inner voice.
I develop my integrity each time I tell the truth.
My integrity is my word, and my word is my truth.
My communication comes directly from my deep center.
I express my love and goodness each time I speak.
My spirit rests in peace and silence.
I trust the whisper of angels' voices as I sit in silence.

mirror, where you can see your whole body. Practice speaking from deep in your abdomen and creating a deep vocal resonance as you say the affirmations. Tell yourself you are all that you know you can be, repeating the affirmations over and over again.

When you have integrated the affirmations into your subconscious mind, you may want to record yourself speaking them. Play a tape of your voice at night before you sleep and let them be absorbed. You can also say them to yourself when you are driving, jogging, or in the shower. Some people even create songs in which they sing their affirmations to themselves. It is always best to speak them aloud.

Try reading your affirmations to others. Ask a friend to stand ten feet away so that you are forced to strengthen your voice. Ask them to tell you if they are convinced by your speech. Practice projecting your voice to them so that they receive the quality of your communication. It forces you to make your affirmations believable.

After you have practiced your affirmations you can also practice silence. Being quiet stills the mind and lets you weigh the things you choose to say to others. Silence also helps us value the words we do use even more. In silence we have an opportunity to listen to angels whispering in our ears. This is how we experience inspiration and guidance. Learning to be comfortable with silence may take practice if you have become used to the noise around you all the time.

Above **Through singing, Sting strengthens his Throat Chakra. He is also comfortable speaking out on subjects he feels strongly about, such as conservation issues. Communicating your truth is how others will come to know your thoughts and feelings.**

Left **Speaking out is the gift of a free society that values freedom of speech. Speaking our truth is what differentiates us from all other life. This is a gift we seldom realize. Express the best of yourself with those who value who you are and respect you for your willingness to share yourself.**

MEDITATION FOR
THE THROAT CHAKRA

Select a candle and some incense. Sit comfortably with your spine

straight and your head resting on top of your shoulders. Take several deep

breaths so that the muscles in your upper back and chest begin to relax. Drop your

jaw and relax your tongue. Feel tension release from your scalp and feel your eyes pulling

inward. Light the candle and burn the incense, and focus your attention in your mouth

and throat. Release any congestion you experience in this area by breathing deeply into it.

Close your eyes and visualize a turquoise blue, inverted pyramid suspended from your jaw.

The apex of this pyramid is pointing down toward your heart. As you hold the image, expand

the form and intensify the color. Feel the pyramid act as a seal that prevents energy

dissipating from your throat and becoming locked in your neck. Feel the tension at the

back of your neck begin to relax and the tension in your throat and tongue loosen

as you fill this area with turquoise light. Feel the energy radiating from

your throat, expanding it and filling it.

visualize a TURQUOISE BLUE, inverted PYRAMID suspended from your JAW

Begin to build the qualities of the Throat Chakra into the

pyramid. Feel the band around your jaw firm up as you acknowledge

the depths of your personal integrity. It contains your commitment to the

truth. The back wall of this pyramid contains the energy of truth, both your

personal truth and the higher truth of God. It feeds energy into your ears so that when

you experience the truth you know that you have been given guidance.

The left side of this inverted pyramid represents your willpower. Your will becomes

strengthened each time you take a stand for yourself or complete a task. Resolve to

complete, in the best way you can, what is unfinished in your relationships. It helps

you stay connected both to the spiritual realm and to the world around you, and

liberates energy that may have been suppressed deep in your Throat Chakra.

The front wedge of this pyramid represents the energy of communication. It feeds your vocal cords and larynx, helping you speak your truth and reach out to others. Choosing your words consciously supports you in making wholesome and rich connections with others. The far right side of this pyramid contains creative energy that helps you express more of who you are. This can be used for art, writing, music, or anything that gives you joy. Creative outlets help you develop yourself. Sit in silence now as you hold this energy in your throat center. Allow your ears to open to the truth and your willpower to strengthen. Feel the creative flow of energy stimulate your mind and your desire to share yourself with others.

Seal this chakra with a cross of light within a circle of light. Let your ears remain open to hearing lovely things about yourself. Know that you hear the truth, you feel it, and you express it. Who you are is truth itself. As you come out of this meditation, take time to be with yourself in silence. It takes a moment to readjust your hearing to the outside world. Be gentle and give yourself a moment to reintegrate your senses to the world around you. You may notice sounds you were never aware of before, such as birdsong, the hum of the wind in the trees, or the sound of water running in a fountain. Pay attention to what your ears are attracted to.

CRYSTALS

TURQUOISE

Highly prized by North American Indian and Asian cultures, turquoise is said to contain the spirit of the creator within it. Use it to increase creative energy in the Throat Chakra. It will heal any tendency to lose energy and help deepen a commitment to telling the truth.

BLUE AGATE

This stone helps anchor your spirit in your body. It helps preserve physical energy so that it is not dissipated in distracting conversations. It assists clear communication, truth telling, and strengthening the will.

AQUAMARINE

This is a beautiful stone that captures the beauty of the sea and the sky. It suggests balanced emotions and a deep commitment to sharing one's true feelings with someone you love for a lifetime of sharing.

QUESTIONNAIRE ON THE THROAT CHAKRA

The questions for the Throat Chakra are centered on your levels of clear communication and conscious integrity. They focus on all the qualities of the Throat Chakra and can give you a guideline to understanding yourself better. If you are timid and afraid of speaking your truth, you may want to look at where this pattern developed and why. If you are an extrovert and enjoy social banter you may want to examine the part of you that never opens to deep feelings and shared intimacy with others.

The purpose of these questions is to help bring you into balance. For some this may involve being more expressive, and for others it may revolve around the quality and truth in their communication. Being creative can help us find our true selves and encourage honesty and integrity. Being congruent in what we say and what we mean is fundamental to establishing integrity. Being comfortable with clear, intentional communication takes time, reflection, and a willingness to come from our core when we share ourselves with others.

Communication

- How willingly do you share your truth with others?
- Do you say what you feel?
- Do you remain silent when you know you have something to contribute to others' lives?
- Do you share your truth with others?
- Are you open, clear, and honest in your communications?
- Do you express your feelings with ease?
- Do you judge others for expressing how they feel?
- Do you become frightened and closed when you have to express yourself?
- Do you know when it is appropriate to be silent?

Right **The scales of justice are a symbol of the weighing of evidence by a judge or jury. Justice relies on integrity and honesty, and these are only possible when we choose to live a conscious life, free from delusion, projection, and guilt.**

Opposite **Turquoise has been highly prized since ancient times and features strongly in Byzantine and Turkish architecture. It is the color that rules the Throat Chakra.**

- Can you be quiet and still when it is needed?
- Do you always need external noise to keep you from your thoughts?

Integrity

- Do you know the importance of personal integrity?
- Do you do what you say you are going to do?
- Do you offer support to others and fulfill your commitment to be there for them?
- Are you truthful and honest in your dealings with others?
- Can you be honest with yourself, even when opposed?
- How do you experience your integrity?
- Do you know when someone comes from their integrity?
- Can you tell when someone is lying and untruthful?
- Are you honest with yourself as well as with people around you?
- How strongly do you value integrity?

Truth

- Do you honor your personal truth?
- Do you tune into your body, your feelings, and your spirit to know what your truth is?
- Do you value the truth of your heart as well as the truth of your mind?
- Do you know when others are being truthful with you?
- Can you hear the truth in yourself longing to be expressed?
- Do you feel a need to cover up your truth with certain people or in particular circumstances?
- How truthful are you when confronted by people who you dislike?
- Do you feel that telling the truth may be offensive to others?

Willpower

- How strong is your will?
- Do you use it for ordinary daily chores?
- Do you reserve your will to meet extraordinary challenges?
- Do you develop will by setting tasks for you to complete?
- Do you feel you need to develop more willpower around exercise and food?
- Do you feel you have a strong will that lets you resolve problems that trouble you?
- Do you surrender your will to a higher will than your own?
- Do you complete tasks that are set in front of you?
- Can you harness your will to develop discipline and wisdom?
- Do you feel you have will developed for challenging and difficult times?
- Do you place your will in the service of survival or surrender it to a higher good?

Creativity

- Where do you channel your creative energy?
- What activities are the most creative for you?
- Do you live from your creative spirit?
- Do you make whatever task is in front of you creative and enjoyable?
- Can you see the connection between your creativity and your spirit?
- How would you be more creative in your life?
- What would you like to develop for yourself in terms of creative output?
- Do you enjoy being creative with your work? At home? In your wardrobe? With your garden?
- Does being creative make you feel good about who you are?

Right **Billie Holiday had the gift of a beautiful voice and was also fond of white gardenias, a flower associated with the Throat Chakra.**

THE COLOR OF THE THROAT CHAKRA: TURQUOISE

This is the color of creativity and self-expression. It is a mixture of the green of the Heart Chakra and the blue of the Brow Chakra. It represents creative spirit and is a color honored by Native Americans and ancient Asian cultures. It suggests the beauty of the sky and universal spirit, and represents all forms of creative expression, communication, truth, and willpower.

Many churches are painted terra cotta and turquoise. The Blue Mosque in Istanbul is made of thousands of tiny turquoise mosaics. The word "turquoise" itself comes from the French meaning a Turkish stone.

The color addresses the spirit and is linked with the vast expanse of sea and sky, which engenders a feeling of beauty, depth, and freedom.

It is a color used to soothe the soul. It is highly prized for decoration, clothing, and any place where beauty is expressed. Turquoise has a calming effect on the body and is said to be able to reduce blood pressure. It is suggested for rooms where people want to relax.

WORKING THROUGH NEGATIVITY

- **Make a commitment to be as truthful as you can in all situations.**
- **Allow your creative spirit to manifest in every activity where you feel comfortable expressing yourself.**
- **Watch levels of substance abuse such as smoking, drugs—both medical and recreational—overeating, and drinking. They weaken the will and destroy the Throat Chakra.**
- **Be careful what you say about others. Gossip can cause damage to others as well as to yourself.**
- **Build your credibility by coming from your integrity. People will respect you.**
- **Listen to your feelings. Know what is true for you.**
- **Listen to what is good, truthful, loving, and kind. It helps to keep your ears sensitive and open.**
- **Speak clearly and mean what you say. Your communication counts.**

THE BROW CHAKRA
AJNA
To perceive, to know

This chakra is known as the control center because it focuses on cultivating a strong and independent mind. It contains the mental applications we need for creating happy and wholesome lives. It is usually fully activated in our mid-thirties when we have accrued some life experience to weigh against the ideas we ingested at an early age. If there has been psychological arrestment due to familial or cultural suppression, this chakra will struggle to work effectively against these mental constraints.

The symbol of the Brow Chakra

Brow Chakra

QUALITIES AND ATTRIBUTES

The Brow Chakra provides the energy for us to experience clear and concise thought, as well as the gifts of spiritual reflection and inner contemplation. It holds the roots for psychological maturity as well as ethical and philosophical principles.

When it is fully activated, this chakra stimulates both hemispheres of the brain. The right hemisphere controls synthetic thinking and creative activity. The left side of the brain controls rational, analytical thinking. Working together they create a harmonious vision of reality that incorporates grounded, logical thinking and intuitive and imaginative experience.

The Brow Chakra provides the energy to expand our inner picture of how we see ourselves and the world. If we cultivate positive beliefs about self and others, our mental picture will be resilient and able to weather disruption.

This chakra is entirely about the power of mind to create our reality at the physical, mental, and emotional levels. It is in the realm of the mind that we transform our lives, harness our vitality, and implement our dreams. The Brow Chakra offers us energy to awaken our minds and question whether what we have been taught is true or false.

To fully activate the Brow Chakra it is necessary to examine self-limiting ideas that denigrate our worth. Its spiritual purpose is to offer us the possibility of wisdom, discernment, imagination, intuition, and knowledge. As we distill truth from life experience, we develop this chakra and strengthen our spirit.

Location: Between the eyebrows

Age of resonance: 35–42

Shape: Five-pointed star

Glandular connection: Pituitary gland

Color: Indigo

Musical note: A

Type of music: Classical, especially Mozart sonatas

Element: The Cosmos

Aspect of intelligence: Control and wisdom

Sensory experience: Mindful knowing/intuition

Essential oils: Camphor, sweet pea, heliotrope

Crystals: Sapphire, tanzanite, lapis lazuli

Aspect of the solar system: The Moon

Astrological associations: Sagittarius, Pisces

Metal: Silver

Earthly locations: Peru and the Rocky Mountains

Mythological animal: Hawk

Plant: Almond blossom

Qualities: Wisdom, discernment, imagination, intuition, knowledge

Life issues: To focus your intelligence; to know who and what are for your highest good and greatest joy; to distill wisdom from your life experiences, both good and difficult; to choose life, health, joy and fulfillment in every aspect of your life

Physical activities: Yoga, tai chi, qi gong, Bates eye exercises

Spiritual activities: Thinking clearly about your life, reading or viewing uplifting and positive books or films, reflection, contemplation, meditation, and creative use of your imagination to visualize the life you say you want

Positive archetype: Wise Person or Elder

Negative archetype: Intellectual

Angelic presence: The Shekhinah, better known as the feminine face of God

ARCHETYPES

POSITIVE: The Wise Person

This is a person who has cultivated wisdom, which the Bible says is more valuable than gold. Wise people offer the best of their life experience to assist others along the path of life. They encourage spiritual pursuits and physical adventures as well as guiding us in making optimally wholesome choices for ourselves. Wise people live by universal principles and trusts in a higher source to guide them through the peaks and valleys of life, and with good fortune they assist us in leading ours.

NEGATIVE: The Intellectual

This is a person who draws only on information from the limited resources of rational, analytic thinking without incorporating either the emotional or spiritual aspects of life. Intellectuals seldom have a holistic assessment of a situation. Their thinking tends to be dry, lifeless, and without energy. They are limited in their scope because they trust only conventional ideas. They are often judgmental and narrow in their outlook.

THE INFLUENCE OF THE BROW CHAKRA

The Brow Chakra supplies energy to all the senses. It feeds energy into the eyes, ears, nose, and mouth and stimulates our sensory acuity. It provides energy to the brain to allow the mind to be active and positive. It opens portals to the higher spiritual realms that surround us and are accessible through developed sensitivity and open-mindedness. New arenas of possibility can be reached through a visionary mind able to think and intuit at the same time.

Above **The bindi is an ancient Hindi sign for the Third Eye, the seat of inner reflection and Divine consciousness.**

THE BROW CHAKRA AND THE PITUITARY GLAND

The pituitary gland is located between the eyebrows in a small cradle in the center of the sphenoid bone. It is traditionally called the "third eye" because it is the seat of intuition and clairvoyance. It is divided into anterior and posterior lobes, each determining a separate function of this master gland.

When people are unable to think for themselves, or experience confusion, lack of mental clarity, and lack of imagination, the pituitary gland may be underfunctioning. It is called the master gland because it secretes a hormone that specifically monitors the activities of the other glands in the body. Its basic hormones control skeletal growth and sexual development and maturation, as well as milk secretion in women. It has a strong influence on thyroidal and adrenal function. It controls blood pressure and is responsible for physical and psychological growth.

When we are deeply attuned to our inner knowing, trusting our intuition and using our creative imagination, this gland works well. When we come up against self-limiting beliefs about our worth and automatically accept them as true without questioning whether they honor who we are, we impede the function of this gland. Our inner state of thought has a powerful influence on our physical well-being, as research is showing, and will affect our hormones and all our ductless glands.

Pituitary gland ....

The power of healing is a function of our minds because it opens us to the good around us. It helps us acknowledge that we are whole, deserving of love and all that we say we want. It helps us expand the realm of new possibilities available to us and lets us see a horizon when we are tired or confused.

The Brow Chakra is especially responsive to both affirmations of our goodness and confirmation of our worth. When we affirm ourselves we actually plant the seeds of goodness into the subconscious mind. They help us reprogram our vision to include greater possibilities for emotional happiness and physical well-being. It is the Brow Chakra that expands as we cultivate a positive, hopeful outlook for ourselves, whether it be in the realm of health, personal happiness, or spirituality. It is here that we first begin the healing process that lets us confirm who we are.

As we expand our minds we learn that wholesome, optimal choices are within our grasp. It helps us to attune our spirit to universal intelligence, which is all loving, all seeing, and all knowing, no matter in what form we experience that intelligence. This universal intelligence responds affirmatively to what we believe about ourselves. If we believe we are worthy of love, goodness, prosperity, and health it says yes. If we believe we are not worthy of what we say we want, or we feel we are ugly and no one loves us, this universal intelligence will, again, say yes. This force attests only to what we believe to be true. This means we need to choose carefully what we want to include in our world-view and examine our belief system to see what is true and has depth, constancy, and grace.

Using wisdom and intelligence helps cultivate the higher mind to choose the good we want in our lives. The freedom to choose belongs to each individual. As the Brow Chakra develops and psychological

maturity is reached, it becomes self-evident that we have the ability to change the way we look at our lives. We can expand the power of the mind to help us create healthier realities. The mind is dynamic and can open the doors to true healing.

The Brow Chakra can control our physical bodies as well as our minds. It governs everything from our heart rate and blood pressure to our ability to withstand pain. Once the power of the mind is harnessed through meditation and yoga, it is capable of restoring health and slowing the aging process. Positive thinking actually increases endorphins in the blood stream. These naturally occurring substances control our "feel-good" factor and help us build reserves of energy we can tap into in times of stress or illness.

As the mind becomes healthier, so does the physical body. When we think positively, situations become positive. We learn to detach from holding onto destructive emotions that sabotage our health and choose to open to the love and light around us.

We can use our mind to develop a healthy Brow Chakra by distilling wisdom from our past. This means we ask ourselves what we learned from a difficult or challenging situation or person.

Another way of expanding the Brow Chakra is to turn the mind off and let it be still. This is one of the functions of meditation. This opens a portal to a higher spiritual realm, where we trust the Source to guide us to freedom, love, and joy. Overusing the mind can distort reality and give us the illusion that we are in control. When we trust the higher mind to work on our behalf we find real and practical solutions for our lives. All the answers to our problems are within us. When we struggle to find answers to our problems outside ourselves, in the world arena, or in the collective mind, we deny ourselves the bounty of our own wisdom.

If we relinquish our spirit or give over our power to choose, we become objects in a game of prescribed formulas and quick fixes, which can control and limit us. These can range from our spiritual practice to medical intervention to impersonal interference in our lives—all of which do not take the whole person into account. When we refuse to think for ourselves, or fail to weigh the pros and cons of any situation, we forfeit our right to make up our own minds.

As we develop the Brow Chakra we are better able to access our internal guidance. We can trust our inner knowing because it comes from the depths of our being. Cultivating the wisdom of the higher mind creates reserves of energy that can keep us healthy and sane for our entire life. Being discerning helps us choose the right path and the right people. Applying knowledge can make our tasks in life easier. Using our intuition and imagination helps us create the best possible life we can.

Besides healing our physical energy, healing the mind is a matter of real consequence. Since this center controls most of what we do in our lives, including behavior, it is important that we develop realistic and grounded attitudes that support our being the best we can be. This is why we try to build a wholesome context for holding our life experiences, forgiving the past, and looking forward toward the light. Healing the mind means reflecting on oneself and transforming self-limiting ideas about who we are and what we deserve.

Above **The Eye of Horus: This ancient Egyptian sign of inner knowing reminds us of the higher power of the mind to access truth, intuitive awareness, and wisdom.**

Below **Walking on hot coals is an act that requires the mind to transform itself from one of limited possibilities to infinite potential. Many people who attempt this find that they can heal their lives by releasing self-limiting ideas about what they can do.**

HOW TO ACCESS THE BROW CHAKRA

The way in which we access the Brow Chakra is to examine how we think and feel about ourselves and our lives. If we are positive about who we are and how we feel about our experiences, then the Brow Chakra will be functioning well and we should have abundant energy available to us to do the things we love. If, on the other hand, we have doubts about ourselves, and a negative opinion of who we are and what we do, it will become necessary to change the way we think in order to assist the chakra in doing its work. This is how we transform our energy.

When we say to ourselves that we are worthless, or diminish ourselves in any way, we fail to honor our magnificence. We, in fact, deny ourselves our natural state of being, which is happy, joyful, and adventuresome. At the same time, we shut down the Brow Chakra and impede it from awakening our mind to the good around us. It is all too easy to repeat judgments that are familiar to us about our lack of worth, or not being enough in the eyes of others. We may have absorbed negativity from parents, siblings, and our community which made self-acceptance difficult and expansion impossible. When we love ourselves we have the compassion of a loving mother and the common sense of a good teacher. We treat ourselves in a loving, kind, and respectful manner. We stay quiet and don't push ourselves beyond what feels right for us at the moment. It is too easy and too familiar to be hard on ourselves. Cultivating a positive and wholesome attitude about ourselves is the first key to healing the Brow Chakra. It suggests being able to recharge our energy when we are tired, re-thinking a solution we are struggling to solve, and being gentle on ourselves when we have had a difficult time.

The patterns of low self-worth show up in the ways people push themselves unrelentingly and how they develop unrealistic expectations to achieve certain goals. When failure to meet high standards makes us feel we are not good enough, we become the harsh and unloving judge.

All these attitudes are lodged in the mind. They are transformed by releasing the past and finding new levels of self-acceptance that are loving, kind, and supportive.

Old patterns can be reframed when we love and honor ourselves. In rethinking our patterns we learn patience, a sense of humor, and compassion. We find hope and faith in life even when things don't go the way we wanted them to.

If we don't change the patterns in our own mind, we give our power to the people who created the negative pattern in the first place, and, essentially, this means we never grow up and live our own lives. Watching

AFFIRMATIONS FOR THE BROW CHAKRA

Repeat these affirmations once every morning and once every evening when you wish to access your Brow Chakra.

I THINK THE VERY BEST

OF MY SELF IN ALL SITUATIONS, AT ALL TIMES.

I open myself to know my inner guidance and deepest wisdom.
I align my consciousness with the source of all life.
I believe I am unlimited in my capacity for joy, healing, and happiness.
I release and forgive the past.
I open myself to new energy, new people, places, and experiences.
I live in the light of my truth and I accept what I know.
I know I am full of God's grace, light, and love.
I create clarity of mind and unlimited vision for myself.
I trust that my highest good and greatest joy are unfolding.
I am wise, intuitive, and aligned with my highest good.
Every situation is an opportunity for growth and healing.
I live in the light of my higher mind and allow it to illuminate my life.
I seek wisdom and guidance in all situations.
I open my imagination to see the best in people and things. I also see the best in myself.
I am the source of truth and love in my life.
As I tap into my inner wisdom, I know that all is well in my world.

Background right **Low self-worth shows in the way we push ourselves unrelentingly. When we fail to meet our own high standards we judge ourselves harshly. We need to learn to be accepting of ourselves.**

our thoughts is an excellent way of being witness to our self-limiting judge who may have the voice of our parents or teachers.

If we choose to move up the ladder of self-love by taking more responsibility for ourselves, we will access higher levels of energy and greater empowerment for ourselves. This is what happens when we change our attitudes.

Should we choose to be fully at one with our life experiences we become the Wise Person archetype. We acknowledge there is wisdom in making mistakes that teach us who we are, and we are tender and accepting of ourselves, as well as nonjudgmental about the things we have done. Each step up the ladder teaches us to love and honor ourselves and to value what we know to be true: that who we are is love, freedom, and beauty itself.

Accessing the Brow Chakra comes when we are willing to think and feel good things about ourselves. Otherwise, any negativity we harbor will shut the chakra down, because it is dealing in half-truths and falsehood. Positive, holistic thinking is crucial to this chakra's function. It is part of our growth and maturation to be able to think objectively and clearly about difficult people and negative situations. This is very difficult to do when we are emotionally enmeshed.

Learning to love and honor ourselves, during difficult times as well as when things are going well, requires us to cultivate wisdom and self-love. Taking the time to examine our attitudes is how we expand our inner reality and let go of harmful negative ideas about ourselves. This can be done alone, in therapy, or in spiritual practices that encourage self-inquiry.

It takes time to learn to cherish who we are and allow goodness to come into our lives. Most people don't even think about the ways in which they abuse themselves until they are tired and run down. If we have had a difficult or unloving past, have made mistakes in choosing less than wholesome people in our relationships, or have been deeply disappointed by life, it could be difficult to change our attitudes. Trust is

Above **The hawk is the symbol for clear and penetrating vision and represents the capability of the Brow Chakra to cut through illusion to come to a higher truth.**

missing and fear predominates. Yet, without this simple act of affirming our worth and the choices we have made, we will remain stuck in the past. Forgiving the past helps us release it and helps us find the serenity to live in the present knowing that we are worthy in every way of a good life.

This chapter offers three specific techniques that help open the Brow Chakra and help reprogram the subconscious mind. They include affirmations, a meditation on the Brow Chakra and its qualities, and the use of questions to probe levels of truth about who we are. The questions will help you evaluate what degree of development your Brow Chakra has reached.

MEDITATION FOR
THE BROW CHAKRA

Begin meditation by sitting in a place where you feel comfortable and
safe to explore your inner reality. You can light a candle or burn incense if you
choose. Begin to relax by letting your eyes sink deep into your skull and let your
tongue relax in your throat. Release tension in your jaw by relaxing your chin, and let your
shoulders drop as you take several deep, relaxing breaths. The more you can attune your
attention to your breath, the easier it is to slip into a meditational state where the mind is still
and you experience peace all around you. When you feel receptive, begin the meditation for
the Brow Chakra. It is designed to activate the qualities of wisdom, knowledge, intuition,
discernment, and imagination. It will help you to focus on the truth of your experiences
and put you more deeply in touch with your own true nature. As you relax, visualize
a large, indigo blue, five-pointed star. Locate this in your Brow Chakra, between
your eyebrows. Expand the form and intensify the color.

VISUALIZE an INDIGO BLUE, five-pointed STAR located between your EYEBROWS

Go through each one of the five points and designate them
as wisdom, discernment, imagination, intuition, and knowledge. Feel
the flow of energy move through each one of the points. It will expand the
chakra and open your mind to developing these qualities within yourself. You can
reflect on each one of these qualities by itself and visualize how it would manifest in
your life. For instance, how would wisdom help you in a particular situation? How would
you use discernment if you could develop it? What would you know if you allowed your
intuition to guide you? What type of knowledge would help you through a difficult time?
How would you imagine your life in five years time?
Allow the light from this star to expand and fill your entire head with a soft light that
permeates your interior space. This is the light of consciousness, which will bring
you peace of mind and inner knowing. It is the light of truth, which
expresses your deepest longing for oneness, love, and beauty.

Let this light fill the dark recesses of your mind as you allow it to expand and fill you. See the beautiful, rich blue light fill your eyes, ears, nose, and mouth and cover your entire face and skull. See that light filling your head and cooling off any agitated emotions or sense of frustration you may be feeling. Allow this light to run through every nerve ending in your brain and cool you off and give you a deep sense of balance and well-being. Give yourself permission to sit quietly and explore this light of consciousness for several minutes. Are there images that come to your awareness, or words? If they repeat themselves they may hold an important message for you. If any images appear in your mind's eye while you are meditating, allow them to be there; simply notice them and give them space. As you practice this meditation it will become easier to focus your attention and concentrate on this inner light. When you are ready to complete this meditation, visualize a cross of light within a circle of light sealing and protecting the Brow Chakra. This will seal in the energy that you have opened up from practicing this meditation. As you practice more often, you will find your mind is clear and receptive to ideas that can support you in your life development. You will feel restored and calm after doing this for a few minutes daily.

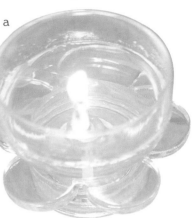

CRYSTALS

SAPPHIRE

This is a precious stone that contains the truest blues. It is a stone that stands for fidelity in relationships, clarity of thought, and a decisive mind. It can be used to sharpen the mind and lift the spirit. It is often chosen for wedding rings.

LAPIS LAZULI

This stone is known as the Philosopher's Stone, because it contains the colors of truth and integrity. It represents the wisdom principle of the higher mind. It can be used to create a spiritual context for holding one's life's experiences.

TANZANITE

This stone is the most beautiful shade of blue because it contains more violet than sapphire in it. It is also more costly now because it comes from only one mine, located in Tanzania. This stone can be used for healing, and stands for one's commitment to expressing truth and wisdom and love.

These questions are designed to help you see what areas of your Brow Chakra need attention and focus. You can do these questions with friends or family to help you, or you can do them by yourself. Either way, they will help you make internal connections with yourself. They will touch deep and uncharted parts of your psyche, which may stir up longing to understand yourself better. Looking within can help you come to grips with aspects of your personality that you may have suppressed or not understood before. Allow the questions to bring up issues that need some attention. It is part of growth and healing.

Ask your higher self to reveal the truth of your experience to you. Be patient for a response. These questions can give insight and healing.

Wisdom

- How wise do you feel about your life?
- What do you know that you know?
- Do you respect the wisdom that comes from the life experience of your friends and elders?
- What is your personal wisdom about your health, happiness, relationships, finances, sexuality, and healing?
- Do you feel safe sharing your wisdom with others?
- Do you listen for the wisdom people share with you?
- Can you look at the challenging experiences in your life and distill wisdom from them?
- In your wisdom can you forgive the past and extract the learning that was there for you?
- Can you find the wisdom to love and accept yourself after a difficult day or experience?

Discernment

- How do you discern what and who are for your greatest good?
- Do you let others drain you because you cannot discern a healthy boundary? Or because you want to please others at the expense of your peace and happiness?
- What are your criteria for discerning whether someone is trustworthy and has the potential for being a friend?
- What are your criteria for discerning truth from hype?
- Do you trust your ability to discern good from bad, mediocre from wholesome?
- Are you able to say no to what is not good for you? Can you discern those who are on your side and those who are exploitative and manipulative?
- Do you find yourself in situations where you have failed to be discerning and then have to back away because you know you are in over your head? Or that you may have let others invade your innermost thoughts and feelings?
- Can you allow yourself to look at the situations and people in your life and draw a line to protect your health, resources, and spirit from being abused and hurt by those who do not cherish you?
- Can you discern what is really valuable and beautiful about yourself and honor that within you?
- As you develop discernment can you trust your ability to know what is good for you?

Knowledge

- Do you value knowledge that can make your life more fulfilling and meaningful?
- Can you distinguish between knowledge and information?
- Are you willing to take time to accrue knowledge about the things you love and enjoy in life?
- How important is learning to you?
- Would a refined and qualitative form of knowledge make your life better in a some essential ways?
- What areas of your life would you like to develop by gaining more knowledge?
- Do you respect your ability to learn and stimulate your mind with good books, films, and interesting experiences?
- Knowledge is a survival tool for your soul. Are you able to know what is important to know and what is a waste of your time and energy?

Imagination

- Do you allow yourself to daydream about what your life would be like, if only...?
- Can you visualize what your life will be like in one year? Five years? Ten years?
- Imagine what you would be like if you had your dreams realized. What would be different?

Left **We use our intuition to tell us the inner truth about a person or situation. When we learn to trust our intuition we are guided by the inner light of Self.**

Right **Our minds are inundated with too much low-level information. Learning to discriminate what is important frees the mind to find balance and harmony.**

- ◌ What are the things in your life you would like to see improved? What would it look like if they were realized? Can you imagine yourself happy with the changes that are presently taking place in your life?
- ◌ Can you imagine being loved and cherished in a way that respects who you are?
- ◌ Can you imagine being financially stable with enough money to do what you want?
- ◌ Can you imagine having a level of health and vitality where you have the energy to do what you love?
- ◌ Can you imagine a level of gratitude where you are completely at one with the creator and know exactly where the goodness in your life comes from?

Intuition

- ◌ How do you know what you know?
- ◌ Do you ever allow your intuitive powers to show you a future, or the true nature of a person or a situation?
- ◌ Can you trust what your intuition tells you about something or someone?
- ◌ Are you willing to tap into the storehouse of knowing available to you?
- ◌ Can you use your inner knowing to intuit what is best for you?
- ◌ How do you use your intuition at present? Do you ever know that something is the way it is, regardless of what others try to tell you?
- ◌ Do you trust psychics and clairvoyants to tell you what they intuit for you? Would you trust yourself to know what is opening for you?

THE COLOR OF THE BROW CHAKRA: INDIGO

This is the color of universal healing. It stands for detachment and represents a cool and clear level of consciousness. Indigo is the color used to unblock congested energy in parts of the body and works well to reduce a fever or blocked emotions. It can reduce levels of inflammation that are festering and cool down stressed-out nerves. It is the antidote to frustration and anger.

Indigo brings our awareness to a higher plane by opening our consciousness to what is limitless and expansive. When we visualize blue we raise our vibrations to a high tone. It connotes lucid thought processes and detached emotions. Rooms painted in this color feel and appear to be larger. It has been shown that after vigorous exercise a person cools down quickly when in a blue room.

Indigo can also seem cold and lacking in human warmth if not counterbalanced with yellow or orange. It can leave us too detached and feeling emotionally disconnected. It is cool, antiseptic, and unearthly because it is the color of spirit, the higher mind, and clarity.

WORKING THROUGH NEGATIVITY

- ◌ **Allow your mind to relax. Overuse leads to worry and obsessions.**
- ◌ **Be willing to move past quick fixes and shallow and superficial solutions.**
- ◌ **Question anything or any person who negates your innate worth, sense of freedom, or beauty.**
- ◌ **Look for the good in each person and each situation.**
- ◌ **Note any abusive patterns in your life and tell yourself, "Never again."**
- ◌ **Stop comparing yourself with others. Find what is unique about you.**
- ◌ **Meet like-minded people on courses and in workshops. Doing so can assuage fear and loneliness.**
- ◌ **Read and see uplifting and inspirational books and films.**
- ◌ **Look at yourself daily in the mirror and feel love for yourself.**
- ◌ **Make a choice to be as loving and positive as you know how to be.**
- ◌ **Be aware when you are tired and weary. Do something positive for yourself.**

THE CROWN CHAKRA
SAHASRARA
Thousandfold

The Crown Chakra reaches the heights of spirituality. It connects us with our indelible and permanent divinity, and is the source of healing energy in the human energy system. The chakras act as a ladder to love, spirituality, and healing, from the base energy of the Root Chakra, which anchors us in life, to the more refined spiritual energy of the Crown Chakra. Like all other energy centers in the human energy system, the Crown Chakra exists as a vestigial core of potential until it is activated.

The symbol of the Crown Chakra

Crown Chakra

QUALITIES AND ATTRIBUTES

The Crown Chakra opens when we have attained psychological maturity and spiritual development. The opening of the Crown Chakra coincides with a time in our lives when we may have to face several difficult personal choices and external life challenges. These ultimately bring us spiritual insights and a greater sense of what we are capable of, and what our higher purpose might be. For many, such realizations are often seen as a form of "midlife" crisis—enlightenment often leads us to reject what we have been, in pursuit of what we could become.

The Crown Chakra is the center where we experience and know a higher god as an active presence in our lives and where we can choose to follow his ways. It is the driving force for mystics and healers immersed in cosmic consciousness and for all those who actively seek and cultivate their spiritual path.

In order for the Crown Chakra to open, it is no longer necessary for us to renounce the world and its material temptations entirely. Our goal must be to see the spirit in all life and to understand that we are here on Earth to be happy and fulfill our soul's longings for love, peace, and happiness. When the Crown Chakra does open, we need rest, tranquility, and peace in order to contemplate the wonders and mysteries of the divine. By balancing worldly activity with spiritual pursuits we can remain grounded in life, often bringing healing and transformation in subtle ways to our immediate world.

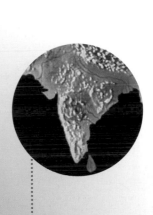

Location: Top of the skull

Age of resonance: 42–49

Shape: Round skullcap

Glandular connection: Pineal gland, which secretes melatonin and other hormones known to affect tranquility, sleep, and light sensitivity

Color: Violet

Musical note: B

Type of music: Indian ragas

Element: The Cosmos

Aspect of intelligence: Spiritual understanding

Sensory experience: Bliss

Essential oils: Violet, lavender, lotus, elemi

Crystals: Amethyst, alexandrite

Aspect of the solar system: The universe

Astrological association: Aquarius

Metal: Platinum

Earthly location: India

Mythological animal: Eagle

Plant: Lotus flower

Qualities: Grace, beauty, serenity, oneness with all that is

Life issues: Selfless realization of your indelible connection with the greater whole of life; creation of a vital and resilient spiritual context for holding your life experiences

Physical activity: None—stillness

Spiritual activities: Prayer, meditation, reflection

Positive archetype: Guru

Negative archetype: Egotist

Angelic presence: The Christ Light

ARCHETYPES

POSITIVE: The Guru

Gurus are people who realize who they are. They know that the divine force flows through them and they are identified with that as the substratum of their being, rather than the temporal parts of their life. They let life move through them and take them ever deeper into consciousness itself.

NEGATIVE: The Egotist

Egotists are people who think their efforts alone carry them through life. They believe that they are separate from a greater whole of existence and that their striving and effort controls the outcome of their life.

THE INFLUENCE OF THE CROWN CHAKRA

Left **The bishop's miter represents the divine presence located in the Crown Chakra. Jews, Catholics, and Muslims all cover this delicate and volatile energy center in reverence to a higher power.**

This center eases physical and emotional pain and releases endorphins, which create happy and blissful experiences for us. This hormonal release can be activated through meditation, yoga exercises, and developing a sense of love for beauty and for life. When the Crown Chakra opens, it brings attitudinal changes and a more positive outlook toward life. It helps a person develop a spiritual context for challenges and difficulties. It induces both gratitude and acceptance. The rule of the ego, which is the part of us that divides, limits, and judges, no longer has dominion over the mind. Instead, there is compassion and a sense of oneness with life and an acceptance of one's self.

Healing happens when the mind is loving, inclusive, embracing, and allowing. As the Crown Chakra opens we gain the awareness that, although reality may appear to be diverse in nature, it is ultimately undivided, whole, and benign. Our higher mind learns to accept that we are loved, guided, and protected by a source higher and more powerful than ourselves and we are each here for a purpose.

Once we start living from and within the Crown Chakra we start to be thankful for our lives exactly as they are. In having formed a spiritual context in which we can retain our life experiences, we accept the trials and hardships that have shaped our spirit. By realizing that our lives could not be any other than what they are, we are able to relish being exactly as we are now. We know—or are awakened to the awareness—that who we are is divine in nature and nothing can stop our spirit. This mental and emotional transformation supports our audacity for seeking a better life and gives us the inner strength to pursue our rightful path.

Whichever way we experience the divine, we accept that our lives are not in our

THE CROWN CHAKRA AND THE PINEAL GLAND

This gland is located at the top of the head. It resembles the rod and cone of the eye and seems to be light-sensitive. It controls sleep patterns, menstrual cycles, and deep rhythmic cycles of the body. It is associated with higher consciousness and is the realm of the divine.

We activate this gland when we do meditation, yoga, and self-realization inquiry. It is felt to be our link with cosmic energy, which enters the physical body through this chakra and stimulates this gland.

It is known that in certain Eastern esoteric practices, focus on the pineal gland opens the higher mind to illumination and a sense of oneness with all things.

·········· **Pineal gland**

hands alone. By surrendering our fears and burdens to a higher power we are able to cope better and more calmly with any pain, loss, or separation we may encounter. When we begin the process of conversion—of accepting that our lives are divinely guided— we lighten up, become healthier and more resilient, and open up to new realms of possibilities for living as we would like.

The more we attune our awareness to the ultimate truth of a higher power, the freer we become to live in joy, harmony, and serenity. Honoring the spirit permits us to experience gratitude for who we are and how life unfolds. We learn we are never alone and that we are guided, loved, and protected at all times.

Above **The headdress of a Native American chief marks a particular state of enlightenment associated with the Crown Chakra. A brave traveling the path to wisdom bears only the single feather.**

Left **Sadhus live totally at the mercy of the divine. They renounce material comforts and trust that God will provide them with what they need to survive. They offer blessings and healing to all who give them their daily bread.**

HOW TO ACCESS THE CROWN CHAKRA

Many practices attempt to maximize the spiritual and psychic powers associated with the Crown Chakra. Such practices include purposeful solitude, deep reflection, silence, prolonged fasting, all-night prayer vigils, and visionary quests alone in nature. Such techniques have been used since ancient times to fortify an internal spiritual connection to the divine. The ultimate aim of this was to achieve a higher realm of consciousness in which bodily needs and emotional longings could be eliminated.

Since energy from the Crown Chakra is such a highly refined fuel for the soul, it focuses on attunement to the highest cosmic vibrations. These practices of spiritual purification need to be done privately,

without fear of disturbance, exploitation, or manipulation, and, in the past, monasteries, cloisters, and similar sanctuaries provided the ideal environment for this. Today, when people seek a higher spiritual awareness, it is important they create psychic protection around themselves to keep the precious energy intact. It is very delicate and requires basic grounding techniques to ensure stability.

WHAT YOU CAN DO

Staying grounded in your body helps to stabilize the Crown Chakra. Eating wholesome foods, drinking unchlorinated water, and getting plenty of rest and exercise are ways of staying stable as this chakra unfolds. Daily practice of prayer, meditation, reflection, yoga, or tai chi helps ground the spirit. It is essential to remain stable through all the changes if spiritual energy is going to manifest in your relationships and work.

Never try to force open this chakra—like the lotus, it will flower naturally, when you are ready to accept it.

Top **This mandala is a representation of the self. It is often seen in churches and temples to describe the compellingly beautiful nature of our inner being. It is an aid to meditation and can be used as a tool for entering the inner realms of peace and being.**

AFFIRMATION FOR THE CROWN CHAKRA

Repeat this affirmation once every morning and once every evening as you enter a period of Crown Chakra enlightenment.

GOD IS IN ME,

ABOVE ME, BELOW ME, AND AROUND ME AT ALL TIMES.

God is in me, above me, below me and around me at all times.
I seek the highest truth and the most healing ways to live my life.
I honor and protect my divine spirit.
I know that all is good despite appearances to the contrary.
I look within where I am safe, loved, and protected.
My spirit is eternal. It loves beauty, harmony, peace, and joy.
I trust that my highest good and greatest joy are unfolding now.
I am grateful for all the good things and people in my life.
I accept who I am and honor the spirit within me.
I live in joy and gratitude for the goodness that fills my life.
I appreciate the beauty of Earth and will honor and protect it
as well as I can.
I know my higher purpose is being fulfilled now.
I trust God to show me the next step in my process.
Goodness and joy are mine in all situations.
I am thankful for the awareness and insight I have into the profound
mystery of life.
I honor all people, all religions, and all spiritual paths. Each leads to God.
Thank you for my life, for who I am and for what you have allowed
me to become.

INSPIRATIONAL STATES OF HOLINESS

The power of the Crown Chakra reaches its highest level of attainment in a state of awareness known as Samadhi. This refers to union with the Godhead where the individual ego dissolves into the universal force, becoming one with it. This is like a river discharging its water into the sea.

Samadhi, or Enlightenment, as it is referred to, is that state of grace where a person experiences the oneness of all life. This encompasses all beings, and goes beyond time, space, or our waking three-dimensional reality. It is the most elevated state of awareness known to human consciousness because a person is linked directly with the source and becomes one with all that is. At this level there is no separation between self and other, because all is seen as self.

With this awareness comes the choice to identify with this eternal and permanent bed-rock of consciousness or with the superficial and changeable nature of life. When people have achieved a state of Enlightenment they know their spirit is eternal, unblemished, and always at peace. Allowing life to unfold without attachment or detachment and not identifying with anything, even the state of bliss that accompanies Enlightenment, is the sign of one who has achieved Samadhi.

Above and left **Monasteries, cloisters, and ashrams provide the peace and simplicity for reflection on the inner self. They act as sanctuaries for the spiritual to retreat from worldly temptation and allow attention and concentration on all things divine.**

MEDITATION FOR
THE CROWN CHAKRA

Visualize a violet skullcap sitting on top of your head. Expand the form of the cap and intensify the color. Feel the healing quality of violet surround you like a protective cloak against pain, discomfort, and suffering. As you begin to feel the energy of this color, take a deep breath to inhale its healing properties. Begin to reflect on your breath. As you breathe in, call in the joy that you deserve. As you breathe out exhale what is old, tired, and stale in your life. Keep this up for a few minutes. Reflect on all the joyful things around you: the stars at night, the moon in her beauty, the sun in its splendor. Know how healing the rain can be as it turns the leaves green. Feel the air around you, see the faces of people whom you love and enjoy. Keep your breathing focused on letting this joy into your life and releasing any negative influences. As you open your higher center, take a moment to give thanks for your life.

VISUALIZE a violet SKULLCAP sitting on top of your HEAD

Even if your life does not appear to be the way you would like it to be at this moment, acknowledge that you are grateful to be here experiencing the wonders of your higher mind. Take a few deep breaths and allow your consciousness to turn more inward. Release the events and experiences of the day, or the emotions that you have been attached to for one reason or another. This realm of pure consciousness is one of being, ease, stillness, and sweet surrender to the moment. You need do nothing. In this space all is light, love, joy, and the tender awareness that you are one with all life. In being your self you are free, intelligent, beautiful, and the source of power in your life. When you access the self there is nothing to do but be. Allow the light of love, healing, and peace to embrace you, and pull your awareness deeper within. Feel your body awareness begin to fade away. Feel your thoughts disappear. Be aware of your breath, your heart beat, the stillness of your mind. You are the witness of your own life, unfolding as each moment melts into the eternal now. Keep your breath focused on allowing joy into your life. When you feel saturated by the positive energy that is filling your field, take a moment to seal your Crown Chakra with a mental cross of light surrounded by a circle of light. This symbol will seal and protect the Crown Chakra until you are ready to do this meditation again and allow more goodness into your experience. As you come out of the mediation allow a sense of peace and detachment to carry you through the day. Find beauty wherever you can. Try to look for it when situations are difficult. You will find it. Remember all joy and goodness are yours now and forever.

CRYSTALS

AMETHYST

This stone is associated with the Crown Chakra because it brings spiritual clarity and love of the higher mind. It can be used in healing to diffuse pain.

ALEXANDRITE

This is a rare stone that is highly charged with a highly refined electric energy. It stimulates psychic gifts such as clairvoyance and clairaudience and opens up the higher centers of awareness.

QUESTIONNAIRE ON THE CROWN CHAKRA

The qualities of the Crown Chakra are spirituality, beauty, and bliss. Look at these questions and see how you can develop or strengthen your connections to this most powerful energy source. As you read the questions ask yourself if you need anything, other than your own awareness of self, to be spiritual. You may find that you question organized ritual that limits your personal power, creates guilt, and takes away your personal sense of divinity. Being spiritual requires an openness to knowing who you truly are. This self is to be experienced, not defined, and is something that you come to love, know, and trust in relation to all that is impermanent and temporal.

The self asks you to expand your limited vision of your personality to a higher dimension of awareness where you are an aspect of divine consciousness itself. Developing selfhood requires that you penetrate the illusions of limitation, the negative projections others use against you to make themselves right, and your own negativity about your worth. When you know that God lives within you there is nothing to do but celebrate your life by honoring what is good, loving, trustworthy, truthful, and beautiful.

When you surrender to the self it will sustain you, guide you, and open the doors that you need to fulfill your higher purpose in life. When you come to know that the self is who you are then you can choose to celebrate your life. There is a joy and lightness that come when you develop a strong and resilient connection to the self.

Spirituality

- Do you have a spiritual context for holding the difficult and challenging experiences of your life?
- Can you open yourself to the love, guidance, and protection of a force greater than your limited self?
- Do you feel connected to the Ultimate Reality?
- What are your highest spiritual truths about yourself, life, death, and change?
- Are you capable of changing any negative ideas that limit your sense of oneness with all life?
- Do you empower religion, the Church, a guru, clairvoyants, or healers to give you the answer to life?
- Do you feel that you have to do things to be loved or accepted by the source?
- What do you empower to connect you with that which is already a part of you?
- By doing rituals, chanting, meditating, fasting, or prostrating yourself do you know the source any better?
- Do you feel you can be loved, healed, and cherished by simply being yourself?

Beauty

- Do you find beauty stimulates your appreciation for life?
- Do you allow your own beauty to shine?
- Can you see the beauty in others?
- When you are around dysfunctional or ill people can you see their inner beauty?
- How beautiful do you make your surroundings?
- What is the most beautiful thing in nature you have witnessed?
- Can you see that beauty is part of the wonder of life?

Bliss

- Do you need anything to happen to feel your bliss?
- Do you need to solve the problems of your life to feel your bliss?
- Do you need others to change in order to feel your bliss?
- Do you need to receive anything in order to feel your bliss?
- Can you create the time you need to be still and feel your bliss?
- Can you let go of all external conditions being right for you to feel your bliss?
- What do you need to do to allow your bliss to be a part of your experience?
- Are you willing to give up your attachment to the negative things in your life to be in bliss?

Opposite page **Dancing connects us with the higher realms of the divine. It is said that Lord Shiva danced the world into creation. Each time we experience joy in our own natural state of being, we strengthen the link to God.**

Below **Being spiritual requires an openness to knowing who you truly are. Meditation can help you connect with your inner self.**

THE COLOR OF THE CROWN CHAKRA: VIOLET

This is the color of cosmic awareness. It is known as an antiseptic color that can soothe pain and relieve tension in the body.

Violet acts as a shield against negativity and is a protective color for those seeking spirituality. It is felt to help dissolve the ego. For people who have a fragile ego this color can cause confusion and disorientation. It is always best to balance it with its complementary color of yellow, which stands for a strong sense of self-identity. It is a good color to use for elderly people because it resonates with their stage in life and is not a stimulant. It has been used to help people who suffer from epilepsy and alcoholism, as it regenerates the Crown Chakra.

WORKING THROUGH NEGATIVITY

- Open your awareness to a higher power than your limited everyday self. There is a higher self, which can guide your way, and offer you love and protection. Take the time to find this within yourself.
- Look inside yourself to discover who you are. Release limited ideas of self so they fall away easily.
- Try not to identify with what has name and form. This is limited and is not who you are.
- Read scripture and spiritually uplifting books.
- Avoid becoming entangled in situations or with people who reject peace.
- Explore your true beliefs about life. Don't accept what has been handed to you without knowing whether it is right for you.
- Direct your awareness inward for a moment every day to connect with the part of you that is eternal and indelible. It will guide you through your life if you allow it to.

CHAKRA
healing

Learning how to heal your chakras gives you the power to bring balance and joy into your life. Once you take responsibility for how your energy is, you can use light, thought, and energy medicine to restore health at all levels.

^{AN}INTRODUCTION TO

This chapter covers the many healing modalities you can use to bring healing and balance to the chakras. Consider which methods you wish to explore more thoroughly. Working on the chakras can be done from a variety of healing methods, and all can be effective. The one you feel the most attracted to may bring the best results. Read through the different methods carefully and consider which treatment will benefit you; then wisely allow it to work its course.

Remember that, in the beginning, there may be no visible effects that allow you to say a condition is improving or that you are better. In the realm of subtle energy you will have only your experience to attest to the degree of healing that has occurred. You may feel a greater sense of well-being and joy. Your outlook toward others, toward yourself, and toward the situations you are in may shift so that your perception is more positive and your spirit is uplifted. This is known as being well in yourself. This is how subtle chakra healing works. It asks that you be aware of yourself and notice how you are feeling. Cure happens from the inside out and from the top down. You may notice inner changes before you see external change. When symptoms shift from the top of the body and move down toward the legs and feet, they are following the Law of Cure. This is an ancient law which governs how physical symptoms leave the body.

Right **This geyser perfectly describes how energetic healing breaks open what is congested, imploded, and suppressed. Energetic healing allows us to be more of who we are without cutting off our will or dulling our mind. It is one of the great rediscoveries of our time that energy can be used to bring healing and balance to our fragmented lives.**

CHAKRA HEALING

Staying attuned to your energy levels will be important throughout the healing. While you are healing, there may be times you feel exhausted and in need of rest. This is a time to allow the body to release old, stagnant energy. You may need several early nights and even naps to help the body regenerate itself. You may feel emotional and in need of a good cry or to express anger or rage. Whatever has been suppressed will find its way to the surface of your consciousness. Allowing the truth of your emotions to be apparent will help you heal. It will release congested energy in the chakras and open the way for you to receive your highest good.

When we are in the process of healing, it is important to be aware of dreams and the metaphors they represent for the situations in our lives. Dreams carry psychological content that can unlock our energy system. Keeping a journal during your healing can help you to remember your dreams and the important insights you may receive. You may see a sequence of messages before you as you allow your dreams to unfold and reveal important revelations to you.

In order for the body to redress old wounds and restore balance, it may need to release toxins. This can be done through diarrhea, fever, a cold and sore throat, or flulike symptoms. Allow the body to let go of whatever it needs to without high levels of drug suppression. You may wish to use homeopathic remedies, herbs, or acupuncture to help you through these crises. These are all energetically based medicines that will restore your body to balance without suppressing the detoxification process.

On an emotional level, you may find that you feel irritated, low spirited, or angry for a few days. If this is something that you have avoided experiencing, then allow your feelings to act as a barometer for your emotional reality. These feelings can often guide you to great insight and healing if you give them space. Irritation is a life sign and an indication that something is occurring internally to redress balance. The more symptoms appear on the surface of the body, the more the detoxification process is occurring. Do not suppress rashes, pimples, or other skin conditions. If they do not disappear within a few days, consult your healer. They are often a sign that toxins are being discharged from the deep organs.

The different healing modalities vary in their intensity. Some may need to be repeated over a period of time; with others you will notice that you feel more positive immediately. Being consistent with a therapy helps it to work on your behalf. Changing a modality too soon and not allowing its action to work on your energy system diminishes its effects.

In the realm of energetic healing you may become aware of moods and a change in cycles such as sleep, menstruation, and appetite. Allow these cycles to balance themselves. Sometimes, in order for the body to become self-regulating, these cycles may be disturbed temporarily. Be patient and give your body time to right itself. If, however, you become aware that something is not right after a treatment, consult your physician or healer immediately. Use your own discretion in consulting a healer and know that it is important to be able to depend on that healer when something is changing. You need to feel supported in healing; and being able to discuss your situation with whomever is treating you is a part of all good holistic healing practices.

COLOR HEALING

Color healing has been the traditional way of working on the chakras for thousands of years. It was employed in ancient Egypt and is still used in India today. Because each chakra is associated with a color, sound, and gemstone, these are often combined to help reestablish balance in the human energy system. The principle idea is to match the color with the chakra in need of healing.

There are different ways of bringing the color into the energy field. Some healers use colored silk scarves. They may wrap the body in them or suggest wearing the color on the part of the body that corresponds with the dysfunctional chakra. It is possible to transform the chakra by wearing the color that is needed.

There are healers who project the color from their Brow Chakra into the auric field of their patient. This is done only with imagination and intention. It is very effective for balancing the chakra. As a supplement, holding or placing the appropriate gemstone on the chakra helps release negative energy.

Opposite **Color healing was used in ancient Egypt to bring balance and healing. The Egyptians loved the sun and worshipped its light. They knew that light and color could restore peace of mind, balance the emotions, and release pain from the physical body. We are once again finding new ways to use color to treat some of our most serious imbalances.**

Below **An Indian method of color healing involves covering a pot of honey with a colored scarf so that the honey absorbs the color.**

Color can be employed with the use of pinhole glasses made in the color of the chakra. The eyes absorb the color and send it to the appropriate chakra. This method requires a commitment of ten to fifteen minutes a day for wearing the glasses, but it is powerfully effective.

In India, there are two effective methods of using color to heal the subtle energy field. One is to take a glass pitcher of spring water and cover it with colored silk for the chakra that needs healing. The pitcher of water is put out into the sun so that the color can be absorbed into the water. Then the patient drinks the water every day at the corresponding hour of the chakra. In other words, if it was the Sacral Chakra that needed healing, for example, one would cover the pitcher with orange silk and drink the water between 10 and 11 A.M., the hour of this chakra's optimal energy.

Another method used in India is to place a jar of honey in the sun for a few hours with a silk cloth of the color desired laid over the honey. The color is absorbed into the honey, where it is preserved. A spoonful of this honey each day will help heal the chakra.

Today, modern color healers use a variety of techniques. One method suggests wearing the gemstone, eating the foods, drinking solarized water, and sitting or standing under floodlights with colored filters. These are effective treatments that are noninvasive and gentle. They are excellent for debilitated people and can help restore their vitality and peace of mind without drugs. If, however, conditions prevail, it is important to consult a physician.

HOMEOPATHY

Homeopathy uses the principle that like cures like. It was developed by Samuel Hahnemann in the early nineteenth century in Germany. Hahnemann discovered that a substance that could create symptoms could cure those symptoms using small dilutions of that substance.

Today homeopathy has developed an extensive materia medica that is based on substances, both toxic and nontoxic, that come from nature. These substances are highly diluted to allow any toxicity to be removed. All the patient receives is the quintessential energetic pattern of the substance, and this is used to stimulate the body's natural healing vitality.

Color has recently been included in the homeopathy materia medica. Remedies have been made from light-saturated water using colored gels and mirrors, then diluted. Other ways in which color is used in homeopathy is from the use of remedies that fit into the color spectrum. All substances fit into the color spectrum; therefore, remedies made from these substances fall into color categories. For instance, iron is red and it carries the same vibration as that color. Sulfur is yellow and manganese is violet; they each carry a color vibration that works on the chakras that correspond to that color.

Sulfur, which is a very broad-acting substance, works on the Solar Plexus Chakra and is suited to overactive egos. It is a remedy that brings balance to this chakra. Silica is a remedy used to heal a deficiency of the Solar Plexus Chakra, such as lack of confidence, indigestion, and allergenic response.

Today there are remedies made from precious gemstones that also carry the vibration of a chakra and a color. Emerald, ruby, aquamarine, and topaz, for instance, are now made in dilution to treat conditions that arise in the corresponding chakras.

Right **Acupuncture is an energetic medicine that uses direct stimulation of energy centers to move energy currents up and down the body.**

Above **Samuel Hahnemann proposed the principle that "like cures like." The pillars of homeopathy that he laid down have not changed in 250 years.**

Right **Remedies typically come in bottles with pipettes to measure the tiny quantities required.**

ACUPUNCTURE

Acupuncture—an ancient Chinese procedure—does not relate to chakras as much as to vessels of energy. It works on a system of "meridian points," which correspond to various organ functions in the body. The meridians are linked to chakras by virtue of the fact that certain organs correspond to chakras.

Today in Germany a form of "colorpuncture" has been developed, which uses needles dipped in solarized, colored water and placed on specific points along the meridians. This affects the chakras directly and brings balance and healing in subtle, energetic ways.

FLOWER ESSENCES

The wonderful Bach flower remedies were developed by Dr. Edward Bach, a British homeopath, in the 1930s. Bach hoped to cultivate remedies that would work specifically on the Emotional body. He felt that flowers offered the gentleness required to heal fraught and discordant emotions.

His remedies are made in a different way than a homeopathic remedy. They are not diluted, but made from soaking the flower in spring water and placing that liquid in the sun for several hours. This is called a "mother tincture" and is used specifically to heal emotional dysfunction.

Bach's work opened a pathway for other flower essences to be used for healing. Today the Australian Flower Essences, remedies from the Flower Essence Society of California, and several other regional and national essences offer healing for distraught emotions and physical problems. They work through the chakras by color and emotional affinity.

Top left **Dr. Edward Bach, a Harley Street doctor, created the Flower Remedies in the 1930s. His philosophy was, "A healthy mind ensures a healthy body." He categorized 38 negative states of mind and formulated a plant- or flower-based remedy to treat each of these emotional states.**

Right **Flower essences carry the healing vibrations of plants and flowers to stabilize the emotions and restore balance. They are gentle, safe, and highly effective for treating imbalances in the Emotional body.**

HANDS-ON HEALING

There are different forms of hands-on healing in which a healer will balance the chakras. In general, hands-on healing is done through infusing the subtle body with charged magnetic energy from the practitioner's own field. This helps to release blocked energy that has congested and caused energy stagnation.

A healer is able to read levels of clarity and vitality in the chakra through observing the aura and asking patients to talk about the specific problems in their life. If a person is having problems with love, the diagnosis is clear: the Heart Chakra is blocked. If the problem is the inability to reason or find a path of direction, the Brow Chakra would be worked on. If the problem is physical vitality, the Sacral Chakra would need attention. Some healers see colors, others hear guidance, still others use affirmations to ease distress.

Understanding the chakras and their emotional components helps you to diagnose where there is imbalance and where healing is needed. Some healers begin by asking the patient to lie on a table and begin to relax. They may massage their hands, feet, and head to get the patient to relax and release fears and tension. Crystals may be used to anchor the spirit in the body, making it easier for the patient to remain aware of and sensitive to emotions, thoughts, or pictures that arise during the treatment. This allows patients to participate in their own healing and assist the healer.

Some healers use a pendulum to read the energy of the chakra. This helps determine the degree of congestion and the regularity of movement in the chakra. The healer holds the pendulum over the chakra and watches it gyrate. Even movement in a clockwise direction indicates that the chakra energy is flowing in the proper direction. Movement of the pendulum in a counterclockwise direction indicates that the chakra is blocked and in a negative spin. When this occurs it is suggested that using affirmations can turn the spin of the pendulum back in a positive

Opposite **There are many different hands-on methods developed by healers. All address the subtle energy field to restore peace, movement, and vitality.**

Far right **Using a pendulum helps to locate imbalance in the chakras. It can show you where energy is blocked and where it is flowing. After a treatment a pendulum can show you how you have restored equilibrium in the energy system.**

Below **Massage works on destressing the body so that energy can flow freely. It helps decongest the chakras by restoring circulation, deepening the breath, and relaxing the mind.**

direction. Having the patient repeat healing sentences, such as "I love myself," "I am whole and complete," and "I am a child of God and embraced by his love," can bring balance and healing quickly.

In the course of balancing the chakras, emotions that were previously blocked may be experienced. It is not uncommon to release energy through tears or laughter. Sometimes, when anger is blocked, it may be appropriate to ask the patient to experience rage and anger. This does not mean that patients have to be emotive or act out their feelings. They simply need to feel their emotions.

After the healer takes a reading of the chakras, the patient turns onto the stomach and the healer's hands can be placed on one chakra at a time to balance the energy system. The healer can move her hand back and forth in clockwise circles over the chakra or in a figure-eight motion. This can be done over clothing and even through a blanket.

It can be very soothing and healing to play quiet and gentle music to calm the nerves and still the mind as the healer works on the chakras. A gentle chakra massage releases accumulated energy and opens the field for positive thoughts to be received.

This massage can be done over each one of the chakras. As the healer moves up the body, less time is spent on each chakra. It is advisable to massage the Root, Sacral, and Solar Plexus Chakras for ten minutes each. The Heart and Throat Chakras can be massaged for five minutes each. The Brow and Crown can be massaged for one minute or less. The closer you get to the sensorium, which is part of the nervous system, the less time it takes to shift the energy in the chakras.

After this is done, the chakras are sealed in order to keep their energy field clear

and resilient. The chakra is sealed by taking a small tea light or candle and making a cross of light within a circle of light, moving clockwise around the chakra. This can be done in the front and the back of the body to seal in the delicate and volatile energy of each chakra.

After each chakra has been circled, the entire auric field is sealed as the practitioner moves clockwise around the body three times. This seals in the good, healing energy and protects the chakras. A second dowsing with the pendulum will indicate that energy has been shifted and balanced.

This method of healing varies from other hands-on methods, but it is similar in that they all address the chakra system. For instance, the Japanese system of reiki uses specific symbols to correspond with the chakras. It filters life energy into the chakras for healing and balance using the hands-on method. It relies on intent and love to bring in universal healing energy.

CRYSTAL HEALING

Crystals can be worn or placed on the body to energize or balance the various chakras. They can be found in most crystal shops and must be cleansed in cold water and salt and energized by being placed in the sun or in moonlight. Sun activates the male principle and gives strength, fortitude, and resilience. The moon activates the feminine principle of receptivity, harmony, and openness.

Here are the crystals that are used for the various chakras:

Root Chakra: ruby, garnet, bloodstone, hematite, pyrite

Sacral Chakra: carnelian, tiger's eye, agate, quartz, calcite, rutilated quartz

Solar Plexus Chakra: topaz, citrine, yellow diamond, opal

Heart Chakra: emerald, peridot, jade, rose quartz, ruby

Throat Chakra: chalcedony, aquamarine, turquoise, jade, chrysocolla

Brow Chakra: sapphire, tanzanite, iolite, lapis lazuli, soapstone

Crown Chakra: amethyst, alexandrite, fire opal, labradorite

When healing a specific chakra, the crystals should be worn around the neck, or they are placed over the body, on the chakras, for a quarter of an hour each day. When the healing is complete, it is important to remove the crystals and wash them thoroughly, because they will have absorbed the negativity discharged from the chakra.

Crystals can be kept near your bed or at your desk, or worn around your neck on a chain. They may need to be cleansed from time to time by being placed under cold, running water. If you have worn a crystal for a period of time during stress or change, it is advised to give it time to discharge the negative energy it has absorbed. You can place your crystals in the freezer compartment of your refrigerator for a few days to let them "chill out."

Below **Crystals can be used to stimulate and heal the chakras. They can be carried or placed directly on the chakra or wherever there is agitation or congestion in the body.**

SOUNDING THE CHAKRAS

Sound healing works on a similar principle to that of color healing. Each chakra resonates with a particular note of the musical scale. These notes can be sung, chanted, or chimed over the chakra to discharge energetic dross and open the chakra to a stronger energy flow. Sound is capable of healing our energy field as effectively as color; and, in combination with any one of the modalities mentioned earlier, it helps redress disharmony.

The sounds that correspond with each chakra are as follows on a scale of middle C:

Root Chakra	Sacral	Solar Plexus	Heart	Throat	Brow	Crown
low C	Chakra D	Chakra E	Chakra F	Chakra G	Chakra A	Chakra B

The Indian sitar is designed to bring healing to the chakras because it is tuned to all these notes. Ragas are composed for specific chakras as well as played at specific times of the day when it would be most beneficial to listen to them.

Harp music, too, can be used for healing the chakras, as one note is played repeatedly near the part of the body in need of tuning.

A good voice coach can help you make the specific sound of each note that would allow you to sound the chakras in yourself and for others. Being able to chant these notes is like giving yourself an internal chakra massage.

Below **Harp music has a close correspondence to the healing realm of angels. Each note has a crystal clear resonance with each chakra. Harp music, like the voice, can help release negativity and tune the body for positive experiences.**

Top **Each musical note corresponds to a chakra. Singing holy scripture, as these raga singers are doing, can bring healing, blessings, and grace.**

FOOD THERAPY

The chakras resonate with specific foods that carry a vibration that heals and stabilizes them. When you wish to bring healing to a specific chakra, you may want to change the emphasis of your normal diet to include more of these food types.

ROOT CHAKRA

Meats, chicken, and grains such as wheat, oats, and brown rice are beneficial. Red fruit such as apples, tomatoes, and red berries all carry the red energy of the Root Chakra. Also useful are national or religious dishes that convey community identity. Any favorite food from childhood can also stimulate the Root Chakra and is a reminder of a time the world was safe and carefree.

SACRAL CHAKRA

Fish, other seafood, algae, oranges, citrus, melons, sweet potatoes, squash, pumpkins, and carrots are all good for this center. Dishes that are sensuous to eat and stimulate the memory of good times are also beneficial.

SOLAR PLEXUS CHAKRA

Chicken, eggs, sunflower and olive oils, honey, molasses, pineapple, lemons, grapefruit, and brown rice are all good for this chakra and easy to digest. Food that is good against liver stagnation, such as green vegetables, and foods that aid digestion serve this chakra.

Above **Natural foods that are high in protein and free of additives can aid in healing the Brow Chakra.**

HEART CHAKRA

Heart of lamb, chicken, and beef are good for the Heart Chakra, as are small amounts of wine and sprouts, other greens, and low-fat cottage cheese. Foods rich in omega fatty acids such as salmon are good for the heart, too. The heart needs good nutrition to be strong. It does well with good food that increases circulation.

THROAT CHAKRA

The Throat Chakra likes food that is easy to swallow. It does not like mucous-producing foods such as chocolate, dairy products, or excess sweets. When the throat is sore, lemon and honey are soothing

Above **Honey is known to restore skin tissue, purge the lungs and help digestion. It is used as a medium for herbal essences and homeopathic remedies. It is absorbed easily and can help heal all chakras.**

BROW CHAKRA

In ancient times salmon, tea, and almonds were thought to be good for the brain. Salmon was the fish of wisdom to the ancient Celts. Aristotle said six almonds and tea were good for the brain. Eating lightly keeps the mind clear. Food that is fresh, free of additives, and high in protein is excellent for the Brow Chakra.

CROWN CHAKRA

Fasting is the "food" of the spirit. Occasional fasts at changes of the seasons purify the blood and open the spirit to changing earth rhythms and cycles. Fasting helps us be grateful for the abundance available to us that we are able to choose from.

Left **The very process of grain production from sowing and ripening to harvesting, reflects the bounty of our world. Simple foods such as grain remind us of our connection to the earth and help ground our spirit on the physical plane. Grains bring us the goodness of the earth and help the Root Chakra and Sacral Chakra regain strength, resiliency, and fortitude after illness.**

MEDITATION USING ANGELS, THE GODDESS, AND THE CHRIST LIGHT

The five major archangels, the Goddess, and the Christ light within us offer us guidance as we bring healing to the chakras. If you have a prayer for healing in one or another of the energy centers, offer your prayers to one of these divine aspects of self and allow them to deliver your prayers and intentions for healing to the source.

ARCHANGEL MICHAEL

Michael corresponds to the Root Chakra. He is the conqueror who fights for the good, the leader of the heavenly armies. He stands for courage, integrity, and justice. He is the patron saint of all soldiers, police, firefighters, and others who risk their lives for people. He is the guardian angel of the Catholic Church and the state of Israel. We seek his help to ground our spirit. He brings us the challenge of making our life have purpose and a deeper meaning than merely surviving. He asks us to help and serve where we feel we can offer the best of our talents and abilities to make our part of the universe a better place.

He brings healing to the Root Chakra by helping us belong. He supports us in creating families of choice based on love and friendship, which honors us in growth, truth, and love. He helps us form communities that sustain our spirit. If you have a prayer for belonging, healing your relationship with community, or finding your true path in life, address it to the Archangel Michael.

ARCHANGEL METATRON

Metatron corresponds to the Sacral Chakra. He is the angel who shows us the proper measure of things so that we are able to ascertain what is enough. He rules over appetite, right thinking, and right action. He teaches us to value the material world and to treat our resources carefully and with pride. We call on him to help us know that who we are and what we do are enough. He encourages us to have fun and rest, and

to love life in all its glory. He can help us find our way when we have lost hope and a sense of the joy of life.

When you have a need to pray for health issues, joy, abundance, and a wholesome sense of deservedness, address your prayers to the Archangel Metatron.

ARCHANGEL URIEL

Uriel corresponds to the Solar Plexus Chakra. Uriel is the regent of the Sun and guardian of the gates to Paradise. He represents the power of our own true worth and encourages us to know ourselves. He can be called upon whenever we are in doubt or experience fear or anxiety. He can bring us the healing light of God so that we can find our stillness and know our worth. If you have prayers to help you develop an abiding sense of well-being and to know your true identity, address them to the Archangel Uriel.

ARCHANGEL RAPHAEL

The archangel Raphael corresponds to the Heart Chakra. Raphael is known as the Healer of the Heavenly Hosts. He brings us God's healing love and shows us the herbs and medicines that we can use to bring balance and healing to our system. If you have prayers to mend a broken heart, to know love, and to give your best to those you love and care for, address those prayers to the Archangel Raphael.

ARCHANGEL GABRIEL

Gabriel is the archangel who corresponds to the Throat Chakra. He is known as the annunciator who bore the news of the coming birth of Christ to the Virgin Mary. He teaches us to honor truth by defending it with our commitment to speak up for ourselves, and to oppose untruths. Gabriel teaches us that we, too, can use our voices to heal, inspire, and soothe away pain.

Opposite **Throughout history people have believed in the importance of angels and they have featured heavily in art and architecture.**

Above **A depiction of the prophet Enoch from a 13th-century book of psalms. Legend has it that the Archangel Metatron was once Enoch.**

If you have a prayer to cultivate truth in your life and stop lying to yourself, or stop substance abuse, gossip, or spreading negativity, address your prayers to the Archangel Gabriel.

THE SHEKHINAH, OR FEMININE FACE OF GOD

The Shekhinah describes the Brow Chakra. It comes from the ancient Jewish lore in which the Shekhinah is known as the feminine face of God. We know this to be the concept of the Goddess, who rules over the inner consciousness of life and provides healing, vision, and love. The Shekinah represents this feminine principle. She acts as a figurehead for the Goddess energy which governs this chakra. She helps us to see the inner light in all things and to honor the best part of people. She teaches us to be discerning, intuitive, imaginative, and knowledgeable. She brings us the ability to find our inner wisdom and know our beauty, power, and healing abilities. If you have a prayer to cultivate wisdom and use it for healing, address your prayer to the Shekhinah.

THE CHRIST LIGHT

The Christ Light corresponds to the Crown Chakra. This is the pure light within us that is never born and never dies. It is permanent, ever radiant, and ever connected to the source of all life. When you have a prayer to know your true self in all its splendor, you can commune with that light to request healing, peace, and love. It is ever present, ever responsive to our prayers.

The path to healing the chakras comes with positive intentions, love, faith in your goodness, and gratitude for all that is. The chakras are a ladder of love that opens us up to the infinite possibilities for growth, healing, and creativity. Honoring them through the angels and heavenly Host aligns our energy with spirit and infuses our spirit in matter.

INDEX

The Book of Chakras Index

BIBLIOGRAPHY AND CREDITS

BIBLIOGRAPHY

Wauters, Ambika, **Healing with the Energy of the Chakras**,
The Crossing Press, Freedom, California, 1995.

Wauters, Ambika, **Chakras and Archetypes**,
The Crossing Press, Freedom, California, 1995.

Wauters, Ambika, **Lifechanges with the Chakras**,
The Crossing Press, Freedom, California, 1998.

Wauters, Ambika, **Homeopathic Color Remedies**,
The Crossing Press, Freedom, California, 1999.

Wauters, Ambika, **Homeopathic Medicine Chest**,
The Crossing Press, Freedom, California, 2000.

Wauters, Ambika, **The Chakra Oracle**,
Conari Press, Berkeley, California, 1995.

Wauters, Ambika, **Nature's Healing Oracle**,
Conari Press, Berkeley, California, 2001.

CREDITS

Quarto would like to thank and acknowledge the following for supplying pictures reproduced in this book:

Ann Ronan Picture Library 124; Bach Centre 117; Corbis 65, 85, 116; Gamma/Alain Benainous 91tl; Gamma/Eric Bouvet 89br; Gamma/de Keele/UK Press 78br; Gamma/Buck Kelly 85; Gamma/K. Kurita 93b; Gamma/Markel/Liaison 103t; Gamma/ Jean Michel Turpin 73br; Panos Pictures 104; Penny Cobb 91cl; Rex Features 89; Science Photo Library/Garion Hutchings 12; Trip/Dinodia 14; Trip/J. Garrett 71tl; Trip/M. Jelliffe 42t; Trip/ H. Rogers 32l, 41cl, 45, 61br, 101tr, 101br, 102, 103b, 112, 121; Trip/ J. Sweeney 15; Trip/Trip 51br; Trip/Viesta Collection 43.

All other photographs and illustrations are the copyright of Quarto. While every effort has been made to credit contributors, we apologize should there have been any omissions or errors.

ACKNOWLEDGMENTS

To Rikki Hall for opening her heart to me, Susan Nemchek for her warmth and kindness, love and compassion, Marva Davis, for her profound healing and a depth of understanding, to Dennis Kirchoff and Michael Crumley for fun, great kindness, and brotherhood. Bless you all for making my time with you so rich in love and friendship. I am honored to know you and call you friend.

To the good people at Quarto, especially Tracie Lee for seeing this book through and to Elizabeth Healey for her outstanding artwork. The gift of electronic collaboration has made so much possible.